Diagnostics of Manipulations

Heribert Wienkamp

Diagnostics of Manipulations

Springer

Heribert Wienkamp
Recklinghausen, Germany

ISBN 978-3-662-70434-9 ISBN 978-3-662-70435-6 (eBook)
https://doi.org/10.1007/978-3-662-70435-6

Translation from the German language edition: "Diagnostik von Manipulationen" by Heribert Wienkamp, © Der/die Herausgeber bzw. der/die Autor(en), exklusiv lizenziert an Springer-Verlag GmbH, DE, ein Teil von Springer Nature 2024. Published by Springer Berlin Heidelberg. All Rights Reserved.

This book is a translation of the original German edition "Diagnostik von Manipulationen" by Heribert Wienkamp, published by Springer-Verlag GmbH, DE in 2024. The translation was done with the help of an artificial intelligence machine translation tool. A subsequent human revision was done primarily in terms of content, so that the book will read stylistically differently from a conventional translation. Springer Nature works continuously to further the development of tools for the production of books and on the related technologies to support the authors.

© The Editor(s) (if applicable) and The Author(s), under exclusive license to Springer-Verlag GmbH, DE, part of Springer Nature 2025

This work is subject to copyright. All rights are solely and exclusively licensed by the Publisher, whether the whole or part of the material is concerned, specifically the rights of translation, reprinting, reuse of illustrations, recitation, broadcasting, reproduction on microfilms or in any other physical way, and transmission or information storage and retrieval, electronic adaptation, computer software, or by similar or dissimilar methodology now known or hereafter developed.
The use of general descriptive names, registered names, trademarks, service marks, etc. in this publication does not imply, even in the absence of a specific statement, that such names are exempt from the relevant protective laws and regulations and therefore free for general use.
The publisher, the authors and the editors are safe to assume that the advice and information in this book are believed to be true and accurate at the date of publication. Neither the publisher nor the authors or the editors give a warranty, expressed or implied, with respect to the material contained herein or for any errors or omissions that may have been made. The publisher remains neutral with regard to jurisdictional claims in published maps and institutional affiliations.

This Springer imprint is published by the registered company Springer-Verlag GmbH, DE, part of Springer Nature.
The registered company address is: Heidelberger Platz 3, 14197 Berlin, Germany

If disposing of this product, please recycle the paper.

Preface

Many people manipulate in countless social or communicative situations or allow themselves to be influenced without these behavioral maneuvers becoming consciously recognized by them as manipulation in the true sense. Apparently, the principle "One cannot *not* manipulate!" seems to apply without exception. If this is the case, all additional information on manipulations and how to identify them would be a gain in knowledge that should pay off as protection against being taken advantage of by others in daily life and from which all interested parties could benefit.

After the attempt was made and undertaken in an earlier article to outline and unfold "manipulation as a system," I felt the need "after the work was done" to focus more on diagnostic approaches against the background of "this system" and to search for suitable instruments for the diagnosis of manipulations. Strictly speaking, there are already tried and scientifically examined methods available from both psychological diagnostics and other disciplines, such as the lie scale sometimes included in psychological tests or the lie detector test used by criminologists for truth-finding.

Additional considerations employed by me went further than these previously common methods, if the insight about social influences is correct, that there is not simply the influence or manipulation *in itself*, but rather "a colorful bouquet" of different approaches or facets of manipulation that come into effect, which also play out on different levels of consciousness. For the reader interested in personality-specific issues, the explanations on the differentiation of the construct of manipulation in connection with the differential diagnostic considerations and findings may be particularly appealing, whereas practitioners may benefit more from the behavioral patterns of manipulation proposed and developed here and perhaps test them as hints or indicators in their practical activities, while also gladly taking note of the aids and recommendations for determining "fiction and truth" in interviews. But not only are the manifestations of manipulations diverse, but also their occurrence or manner of appearance in consultations, negotiations, sales talks, and interrogations, to name just the most important ones.

Many "social arenas" are characterized by competition and mutual rivalry to achieve important personal goals. Such critical situations, in which manipulations occur, are not limited to the individual diagnostic perspective with a target person, but they can also exhibit dependencies between the participants and be shaped by these interdependencies. In competitions, for example, in sports, it is usually solely about winning or breaking records, a goal that all participants strive for. In negotiations, although negotiation success in itself is a worthwhile goal, the outcome often also depends on the reactions or approval of the negotiation partner, who also wants to see his or her interests preserved. Strategic thinking and action are therefore indispensable in negotiation situations in order to achieve a balance of mutual expectations. For an analysis of interactions, the question must be clarified as to how strategic thinking and action can be diagnosed within social processes and which concepts and procedures are available for this purpose?

Fortunately, in various areas of scientific research, there are models and instruments for examining social interactions and decision-making problems with divergent preference structures. The game theory is cited as an example. Such concepts can help analyze social systems with their inherent processes, such as moves or strategic-tactical interventions, and make their logic transparent from a higher level. The result would amount to a "system diagnostics" and yield something like a kind of "meta-analysis," taking into account both the current quality of relationships between the participants and the chosen communication paths. "Rational decision-making procedures," as they are often applied in economic issues and optimization problems, in contrast to game-theoretical considerations, follow only their own principles and calculations and focus solely on their own interests and (hidden) preferences in decision-making.

As will still be shown, the "universe" of games or situations involving competing parties striving to realize their respective advantages is almost infinitely large and extends from disputes in the economy through justice and criminology to, not least, politics and society. For the analysis of these problems, it is crucial to determine which principles or needs should be the starting point. For example, is the absolute success or victory at the forefront of events, or should more emphasis be placed on rationality in decision-making, or is fairness or care as social achievements more in demand? It should be understandable that such system-relevant questions or problems cannot be answered and solved in the same way as, for example, in personality diagnostics through psychological tests or the like, but rather require a completely different approach. For instance, in social psychology, the well-known game situations "prisoner's dilemma" and the widely lamented problem of "collective non-responsibility" as a diffusion of responsibility with an increasing number of spectators are very well researched and have enjoyed high attention and popularity, so that a system analysis could also benefit from their research findings.

For rather conceptual reasons, it seems helpful and sensible with regard to the "diagnostics of manipulations" to examine both, that is, both the individual viewpoint and the systemic perspective, and to attempt to track down the manipulation maneuvers "in both worlds" and to investigate their mechanisms and, as well as possible, to diagnose them, accompanied by the desire to gain more insights.

In addition to a synthesis of individual and systemic diagnostics of manipulation attempts, it also seems necessary and advantageous to me to simultaneously consider both "older" insights from previous publications and more recent contributions or considerations on this topic. Older literature sources and "classic" research findings not only deserve the necessary respect of being cited, but they also provide an excellent basis for reflecting on them anew in the light of new assumptions and hypotheses, and for utilizing and further developing them for this topic. Earlier statistical findings (or figures such as correlation relationships) are rather secondary in this context, as they have certainly been relativized by later studies. As far as possible, this contribution includes both cited case studies from practice and my own experiences from my professional activity in personnel management.

I would be very pleased if every reader could benefit in their own way from the explanations on the diagnostics of manipulations.

Recklinghausen, Germany Dr. Heribert Wienkamp
in July 2023

Contents

1 Introduction 1
  1.1 Initial Situation 1
  1.2 New Accents on Manipulation 2
  1.3 Summary 4

2 Forms of Manipulative Behavior 5
  2.1 Impulses for Intensifying Self-Perceptions 5
    2.1.1 Body's Own Neurophysiological Processes 6
    2.1.2 Psychological Processes 6
  2.2 External Observations Triggering Involuntary Reactions or Evaluations 7
    2.2.1 Suggestibility or Influenceability 8
    2.2.2 Behavioral Influences through Prejudices or Stereotypes 8
    2.2.3 Camouflage, Deception, and Hiding 9
  2.3 Systematic Influences 9
    2.3.1 Self- or Autosuggestion 9
    2.3.2 Manipulations of Other Target Persons 10
  2.4 Lies and Other (Supposed) False Statements 11
    2.4.1 Witness Statements Do Not Necessarily Correspond to the Truth 11
    2.4.2 Lies 12
  2.5 Summary 12

3 Behavioral Manifestations of Manipulation 15
  3.1 Behavior Descriptions of Suggestivity 15
  3.2 Behavior Descriptions of Suggestibility 17
  3.3 Behavior Descriptions for Autosuggestions 18
  3.4 Behavior Descriptions for Camouflage, Deception, and Hiding 19
  3.5 Behavior Descriptions for Lying 20
  3.6 Behavior Descriptions for Prejudices or Stereotypes 21
  3.7 Behavior Descriptions for Voyeurism 22
  3.8 Summary 23

4	**Differential Diagnostic Aspects of Manipulative Behavior**			25
	4.1	Construct Validity of the Trait Manipulation		25
		4.1.1	Connections within the Trait Manipulation between the Defined Feature Facets	26
		4.1.2	Connections to Other Personality Traits or Test Scales	27
			4.1.2.1 Connections to general "classical" personality traits	27
			4.1.2.2 Connections to the "Big Five" Constructs	29
			4.1.2.3 Connections to Emotion-Focused Models and Self-Influencing Factors	29
			4.1.2.4 Connections to the so-called "Dark Triad"	31
			4.1.2.5 Personality Tests with a Lie Scale	31
			4.1.2.6 Connections to Prejudices or Stereotypes	33
		4.1.3	Bizarre Types According to the Observations of Theophrastus	34
			4.1.3.1 The Insincere	34
			4.1.3.2 The Rumormonger	34
			4.1.3.3 The Braggart and Fame-Seeker	34
		4.1.4	Noticeable Strange Characters in Our Time	35
			4.1.4.1 The Embellisher	35
			4.1.4.2 The Hasty	35
		4.1.5	And are there more "odd birds"?	35
			4.1.5.1 The Hypocrite	35
			4.1.5.2 The Know-it-all	36
			4.1.5.3 The Worrywart	36
	4.2	Connections to "objective" measures as a sign of criterion validity		36
	4.3	Summary		37
5	**Individual Diagnostics: Distinguishing Between Fiction and Truth**			39
	5.1	Statements of an Affected Person		40
	5.2	Statements of Other Persons as Participants		41
		5.2.1	Statements of the Accused (as "Opponent")	42
		5.2.2	Statements of Uninvolved Persons or Witnesses	42
	5.3	Reactions of Onlookers and Voyeurs		43
	5.4	Summary		44
6	**Manipulation by System**			45
	6.1	Orders and Regulations		45
	6.2	Games and Their Strategic Calculations		45
		6.2.1	Elements of Games	46
			6.2.1.1 Nash Equilibrium	47
			6.2.1.2 Strategy Forms and Moves	47

		6.2.2	Selected Popular Game Types	50
			6.2.2.1 Non-cooperative Games	50
			6.2.2.2 Cooperative Games	52
		6.2.3	Other Game Theory Concepts	55
			6.2.3.1 Balance of Interests through Mutual Agreement or Negotiation	56
			6.2.3.2 Auctions	58
			6.2.3.3 Social Contracts as a Game Concept	59
			6.2.3.4 Looking into the Abyss: Dealing with Dangerous "Cliffs" and Imbalances ("Brinkmanship")	60
	6.3	Summary		62
7	**"System Diagnostics" of Dependency Relationships and Mutual Influence Attempts**			**65**
	7.1	System Analysis and System Diagnostics of the Anatomy of Games		66
	7.2	Selected Games and Their Analysis		71
		7.2.1	Damage Regulation	71
		7.2.2	Failure to Render Assistance	74
		7.2.3	Free Riders	75
	7.3	Other Possibilities of System Diagnostics		77
		7.3.1	Sensitivity Analysis Using "Signal Detection Theory"	77
			7.3.1.1 Basic or Measurement Model	79
			7.3.1.2 Operationalization and Application	81
		7.3.2	Sampling or: "Setting an Example"	82
		7.3.3	Portfolio Techniques for Self-Control and Self-Suggestion	83
	7.4	Summary		84
8	**Economic Concepts of "Rational Decision-Making"**			**87**
	8.1	Theoretical Concept and Methodological Implications		87
	8.2	Application Example		89
	8.3	Other Remarks		91
	8.4	Summary		94
9	**Insights into the Influence on Prosocial Behavior**			**95**
	9.1	Social Preferences in the Assessment of Interactions		96
	9.2	Compassion (Empathy) with Other People		97
	9.3	Summary		98
10	**Implications and Consequences for Practice**			**99**
	10.1	Overview of the Structure of Social Interactions		99
	10.2	Relationship Level		100
	10.3	Communication Level		102

		10.3.1	Consultation	102
			10.3.1.1 Financial Consulting	103
			10.3.1.2 Personnel Consulting	106
			10.3.1.3 Other Consultations	109
		10.3.2	Negotiations	110
			10.3.2.1 Sales Conclusion	111
			10.3.2.2 Balance of Interests	113
		10.3.3	Interrogations	114
			10.3.3.1 Suspects	114
			10.3.3.2 Witnesses	116
			10.3.3.3 Requirements for Evidence in Interrogations	118
	10.4	Summary		119
11	**Therapeutic Applications at the Interface Between Counseling and Treatment**			**121**
	11.1	General Information on Financial Therapy		122
	11.2	Personality Disorders and Maladaptive Behaviors		123
	11.3	Therapy Forms		125
	11.4	Case Example as "Case Study"		126
		11.4.1	Biographical Details	126
		11.4.2	Reason for Treatment and Problem Behavior	129
		11.4.3	Therapy	130
	11.5	Summary		133
12	**Educational Concepts for Promoting Learning, Education, and Personality Development**			**135**
	12.1	Goals and Topics of School Pedagogy and Promotion		136
	12.2	Methods of Educational Diagnostics		139
	12.3	Transfer to Other "Learning Groups"		140
	12.4	Summary		142
13	**Lessons Learned**			**145**
References				**155**

Introduction

The recognition or diagnosis of manipulative behavior is associated with the desire or intention to perceive manipulation attempts in our daily lives at all and, as best as possible, to systematically pursue them, to detect them with a certain level of experience and professionalism, and to expose them. In any case, it should become clear to the addressee and actor of influence maneuvers that their manipulation attempts have been recognized and thus have not led to success.

Typical for all fields of knowledge is that they do not remain at the status quo with their insights based on analyses and attempts at systematization, but are dynamically oriented and continue to develop through ongoing research. The same applies to the topic of manipulation, which, upon closer examination, reveals itself in its diversity and differentiation and repeatedly stimulates reflection and new activities.

1.1 Initial Situation

Without the knowledge of what manipulations actually are and how they can be recognized, that is, diagnosed as such, all counter-reactions and defense attempts probably fail and do not lead to the desired success or miss the target due to ignorance. It is not uncommon for influence attempts to go unnoticed and unregistered as such. When manipulations are mentioned, the general perception is that secret, hidden manipulation maneuvers are meant, which often escape the perception of the target person. But also numerous examples from practice of supposedly harmed individuals who have been "convinced" or rather persuaded to engage in certain activities, such as purchasing an actually unnecessary, perhaps even useless product, fall under the term manipulation and may serve as evidence. This raises the question of what is best to do to avoid becoming a victim of such manipulation attempts oneself?

Manipulative behavior as a system for systematic influence was already the focus of interest elsewhere (see Wienkamp, 2022a) and was presented as a conceivable model. Based on various starting positions, it was possible to outline the different (social) currents, namely to control both one's own behavior through self- or autosuggestion and the behavior of others. Finally, this influence and control system as a preliminary concept also included the possibility of benefiting from other people either to one's own advantage through suggestions, recommendations, and assistance, such as in learning or training in sports, or to one's own disadvantage, if you will, being exploited by egoists solely focused on their own advantage.

Manipulation maneuvers that arise in overarching contexts as "system events" were not addressed and discussed.

1.2 New Accents on Manipulation

Merely the order and classification of manipulative behaviors is unfortunately not sufficient. Additionally, an in-depth analysis of the causes or sources of manipulations, as well as the ability to recognize or diagnose them, should be pursued in order to adequately deal with them in everyday situations. Thus, this contribution is intended to provide further insights, especially in the identification and analysis of manipulative behavior, and to ensure substantial content progress.

It is therefore generally known and conceivable that attempts at manipulation can occur both unconsciously (as involuntary emotional reactions or uncontrolled impulses) and with full intent from strategic-tactical calculations. Fig. 1.1 may

Perspective	Manipulative behavior or reactions	
Self-awareness	(1) Effectiveness of fixed Behavioral programs ("autopilot") as involuntary emotional reactions	(3) Use of behavioral maneuvers for your own benefit and self-influencing (autosuggestion)
External perception	(2) Automatic ratings according to your own preferences or values (e.g. according to liking or disliking)	(4) Statements by other persons about the behavior of target persons, e.g. during witness interviews or similar.
Level of consciousness	*Unconsciously*	*Consciously*

Fig. 1.1 Unconscious and conscious manipulations from different perspectives

1.2 New Accents on Manipulation

summarize and illustrate this systematics of manipulative behavior traits and reactions "at a glance."

Systems or systematics are characterized by the use of schemes, usually through formed orders or artificially created classifications, and the delineation of the components contained therein from one another, as well as by the description and explanation of the interactions between these factors or system parts. Thus, in the already mentioned reading "Manipulation as a System" by Wienkamp (2022a), it was about the variety of manipulation maneuvers. This system of manipulation is based on partly complementary system components of personality traits, such as *suggestiveness* (i.e., the ability to influence) on the one hand and *suggestibility* (i.e., susceptibility to influence) on the other. Or the individual uses related but independent manipulation patterns. Thus, there is also *self-influence* (as *autosuggestion*) or the dependence on *prejudices* or *stereotypes* in judgments and simply *lying* to extricate or free oneself from disadvantageous situations, as often occurs with defendants in an interrogation.

However, merely classifying behavior patterns for the purpose of manipulation into a system created for this purpose is not enough. Added to this must be, on the one hand, a transformation of these behavior patterns into practice with its situational challenges, and on the other hand, it must be examined whether the chosen or developed systematics meets practical requirements. Only then is it to be decided to what extent these manipulative behavior maneuvers can be used for both theoretical concepts and for psychodiagnostic purposes of various kinds, in order to develop appropriate procedures or instruments on this basis.

One of the main focuses of this work will therefore be to treat and discuss the construct of manipulation from a differential diagnostic perspective, in order to distinguish the various facets and circumstances of manipulative behavior from one another and, so to speak, to differentiate between *fiction and truth*.

The aim of the following explanations is to determine which situational circumstances in normal life or everyday life are to be assumed. The attempt is also made to look for special or peculiar personality types who tend to manipulate with their typical and peculiar behavior patterns or reactions and usually incite themselves to do so unconsciously, as is the case with "know-it-alls" who always have to instruct others.

For many "social settings" or situations, it is also true that due to the interdependencies with other people and their reactions, behavior maneuvers occur, or even must occur, that determine or influence the course of events, making it impossible for individuals "not to *not* manipulate," as has already been emphasized elsewhere, when, for example, "a false smile on the face" involuntarily appears as an attempt at deception or distraction (see Wienkamp, 2023a). These behavior traits are particularly evident in games or comparable interactions, where it is either mutually about realizing one's own advantages or interests or about supporting those in need through intended interventions, such as in medical treatments or therapies, which need to be analyzed and examined more closely under diagnostic goals and perspectives.

But also the strictly rational analyzing and acting individuals should be considered when talking about manipulation maneuvers. However, "rationalists" tend to think and act more self-suggestively according to their own methods and calculation methods, rather than being impressed or influenced by others, as is the case, for example, in games.

1.3 Summary

Building on previous work on the topic of manipulation, new considerations and insights should and could be gained based on a system developed for this purpose with the criteria "perspective of the affected person or observer" and the relevant "level of consciousness." As a result, the "picture" of what manipulation actually is and how it manifests in real life becomes more colorful and diverse. Therefore, the focus of upcoming efforts and activities should be on the identification and diagnosis of manipulation attempts.

In addition to individual consideration, i.e., personality diagnostics, system-relevant processes or behavioral traits, such as in interactive games or in connection with social, economic, or political events like conflicts or problems, are also the focus of attention. Both individual diagnostic and system diagnostic questions are of interest and should lead to new insights.

Forms of Manipulative Behavior 2

According to the presented systematics (see Fig. 1.1), both involuntary or unconscious manipulations and deliberately and consciously orchestrated influence actions can be differentiated from different perspectives or with different target objects (or target persons). This distinction is helpful not least because it is possible to determine and diagnose the respective possibility or extent of *self-control* in social influence maneuvers. For it makes a considerable difference whether, for example, a spontaneous involuntary reaction, such as blushing or other neurophysiological signs or symptoms, occurs in response to an attack or intervention by another person, or whether, during a witness interrogation, the interviewee can, so to speak, prepare their statements in their thoughts or in their head beforehand.

There are also quite unspectacular (manipulative) signals that are not perceived and regarded as such. Certain gestures have an invitational character, such as the indication: "Have a seat" or "Take a seat."

Nevertheless, it makes sense to derive and discuss in more detail the possible forms of manipulation and their implementation in concrete behaviors based on this systematics or classification, with the aim of using these manipulative behavior patterns for differential diagnostic purposes and applications (see also additionally Chap. 3).

2.1 Impulses for Intensifying Self-Perceptions

It is simply a fact that in the nature of living beings, fixed behavioral programs are laid out that are oriented towards specific stimuli, which, comparable to an "autopilot," involuntarily control subsequent reactions. These dispositions are genetically determined and part of the genetic makeup. These can be both somatic, more neurophysiological processes, as well as psychological processes of self-perception and involuntary compulsive reactions.

2.1.1 Body's Own Neurophysiological Processes

The best examples of autonomous unconscious reactions are the physical neurophysiological symptoms (or markers) that manifest uncontrollably and noticeably in specific situations. These "somatic markers," as Damasio (1994) called them, are expressions of particular emotional states or conditions. Some people, for example, blush out of embarrassment when suddenly confronted with an embarrassing event, or they feel fear and are startled when they encounter a stranger in the dark, experiencing heart palpitations or shortness of breath.

Emotions are known to represent certain affective expressions or feelings that are not controllable and manageable by the individual but are inherent in nature. It is clear that while the trigger is an external stimulus or event, the reaction is based on an inherent process occurring within the person, which is perceived or felt by the person and to which they are compelled to react.

Apart from these uncontrolled neurophysiological processes, there are also the processes of the autonomic nervous system with the parasympathetic and non-parasympathetic systems, which cannot be influenced by humans, ensuring, for example, breathing and metabolism or the situational adaptation of organ supply under different demands. The autonomic nervous system is also supported by neurotransmitters, which, as the body's own biochemical messengers, like dopamine for sensations of pleasure or serotonin for calming the organism, autonomously and automatically regulate the metabolic cycle.

2.1.2 Psychological Processes

But not only the psychophysiological symptoms fall into this category of uncontrolled emotional reactions. Internal processes of self-perception triggered by external stimuli or people can also become independent and take control over the psychological state and the further process. A good example of this is *voyeurism*, which the affected actors cannot escape, even if they wanted to (see also Sect. 3.7). On the contrary, they eventually experience their momentary satisfaction in the increase or intensification of the excitement triggered by this, which, however, is only temporary and demands further emotional experiences once these voyeurs, so to speak, have "acquired a taste for it."

Voyeurism can become an addiction or a vice when randomly present observers cannot resist the urge and must give in to their automatically arising impulses, such as taking photos of accident victims with their phones. Out of pure sensationalism and showmanship, they then feel compelled to post these phone photos online to spread them and make themselves interesting on social media. Others find satisfaction in eavesdropping on people's conversations or observing and harassing them in their intimacy, such as when dressing or undressing or during other (sexual) activities. This also fits when people are watched by TV viewers out of pure tension and sensationalism in delicate situations for voyeuristic motives, such as watching events in a jungle camp or other TV reality shows like "Big Brother" or similar, and the observers or viewers "delight" in it.

Comparable to voyeuristic drives are imagined desires that involuntarily become independent as (misleading) behavioral reactions. A characteristic of such a psychological mechanism is the statement or proverb by Shakespeare: "The wish was father to the thought!" Inner impulses ensure, with the elimination of any self-control, that a person is inevitably led to false claims, incompetent actions, or even misdeeds, because the impulse, such as greed or desire for something, encounters no resistance. While in voyeurism the urge for need satisfaction is decisive, desires follow a more or less spontaneous inspiration (or even imagination) that forms into a train of thought and pushes for realization.

So-called *"stalkers,"* who follow their former partners at every turn, also cannot escape this inner uncontrolled urge and would likewise belong to this category of uncontrolled psychologically induced sensations and experiences, enriching them, although stalkers do not actually count as voyeurs. The "victims" or target persons are rather objects or trophies taken possession of for these individuals, by no means equal subjects as human beings like themselves.

Well-meaning assessments might assume a pronounced curiosity, provided the behavioral manifestations remain within limits and do not significantly disturb other people's personal development and lives. However, curiosity has nothing to do with a lack of behavioral control and compulsive behavior from a differential psychological perspective. Curiosity seems, in relation to voyeuristic behavioral traits, more of a tendency, at worst a "quirk" or a vice, by no means an addiction.

2.2 External Observations Triggering Involuntary Reactions or Evaluations

Who does not know such encounters or experiences where an initial contact with a previously unknown person automatically triggers either a feeling of sympathy or antipathy as a so-called "first impression"? It is no coincidence that, for example, at information desks, people with a "pleasant aura" are often found, who are immediately likable to others. These felt emotions are also, if you will, "gut-driven" and occur spontaneously and unconsciously beyond our awareness or any cognitive control mechanisms. It should not be surprising that there are again different qualities of forms or manifestations in this group.

The most well-known form is the suggestibility or influenceability of people. In addition, there are weakened mechanisms and reactions that also involuntarily come into play when needed, such as the dependency and therefore necessary use of prejudices and stereotypes or the "deceive, camouflage, and hide," which also automatically apply as an emergency reaction or defensive posture and were by no means initiated intentionally by the actors.

2.2.1 Suggestibility or Influenceability

Basically, we are all somehow influenceable and sometimes even like to be influenced and are even grateful for it because it is so convenient! In nature, the perception of signals by other living beings, such as in animals, is inherent and fixed. Otherwise, for example, emergency calls or warning signals would not fulfill their function and would be insufficient and thus completely superfluous.

Nevertheless, there are interindividual differences in the degree of suggestibility among people. Some are highly receptive to signals from other people, like a seismograph, for everything and are therefore easily impressed and influenced. It can be observed that, for example, a person often agrees with the one they last spoke to. Such people are often unstable and fluctuating in their reactions and seemingly do not quite know what they want and what their preferences and goals are.

Other individuals are the stark opposite, namely stubborn, resistant to advice, and above all conceited and know everything better. Often, there is also an aversion to new, strange, and unknown things. For their fellow humans, it is quite laborious to overcome this artificially pronounced and highly stylized skepticism and to convince them.

2.2.2 Behavioral Influences through Prejudices or Stereotypes

Those who make their judgments and behavior dependent on ideologies, dogmas, or other "unshakeable" principles or beliefs always act automatically according to certain personal but imposed and uncritically adopted preferences, regardless of whether they are appropriate in the respective situation or not. This is due, on the one hand, to a, if you will, "conventional narrow-mindedness" (see Wienkamp, 2022a) both in thinking and in the personal preferences that are never up for discussion, when it comes to taste or practical things in life. On the other hand, prejudices or stereotypical attitudes stem from an authority obedience that forbids or prevents these people from questioning or examining things or matters for their truthfulness. They prefer to blindly submit to their fate. To be distinguished from prejudices or stereotypes in decisions and judgments would be, on the one hand, superstition, which inevitably leads to irrational thinking and acting, and on the other hand, gullibility, which, however, as a personality trait, tends to occur spontaneously and situationally.

It should not be surprising that the use of prejudices or similar leads to perception and judgment errors or enormously favors them (see, for example, Wienkamp, 2022b). This is solely because people with prejudices are guided by so-called "implicit personality theories," where, for example, belonging to a certain social class or group "implies" a certain character or personality profile, that is, it is assumed. On the other hand, they tend to succumb to the "halo effect" or unconsciously apply it in person assessment, when, for example, they assume that people with an advantageous, beautiful appearance are also intelligent, educated, etc.

It is probably not surprising that unorthodox thinking or an open or liberal and tolerant attitude embodies and represents exactly the opposite of prejudices or similar. Such people do not depend on group pressures, clichés, or fashion trends, as they approach every situation or personal challenge openly but also critically.

2.2.3 Camouflage, Deception, and Hiding

When people are under pressure, for example, to take a stand or to present their personal opinion on a topic, they inevitably fear the truth, responsibility, or assumed negative consequences. The only automatic way out for them is to "sneak away" and avoid the situation or reality. They either try to camouflage themselves or hide in a figurative sense, or deceive and distract others, for example, by resorting to excuses.

On the behavioral level, they have various options available. They can embellish their "hide-and-seek game" by juggling half-truths (see also Sect. 2.4); however, they can also omit or leave out important things and keep silent without feeling that they are telling untruths and lying. Other people in such situations are "masters" at dramatizing and exaggerating and simply tend to act or engage in what is also called "impression management."

Individuals who have to deal with such "tricky" people would be well advised to behave in exactly the opposite way, namely to approach with an "open visor" and, even if it is sometimes difficult and may have possible disadvantages or negative consequences, to commit to the truth. They should also pay attention to inconsistencies or affected behavior in their conversation partners and, if necessary, bring this up.

2.3 Systematic Influences

If we follow the goals and purposes of systematic influences, they can relate to oneself, which would be self-influence or autosuggestion, or to another external target person. Regardless of which subject is targeted and aimed at, it is about a desired effect or an influence or manipulation of a process.

2.3.1 Self- or Autosuggestion

Self-influence through self-imposed commands or instructions has the character of self-suggestion and belongs to hypnotic procedures. Most often, self-hypnosis is used in medical-psychotherapeutic treatments (with or without the support of the therapist), particularly to induce patients into a trance or relaxation, that is, into a deep relaxation. Characteristic of a state induced by (self-)hypnosis is the lack of will or the "letting go" by shutting down the left (critical) brain region. With full consciousness and absolute alertness, the process then transitions into a deep relaxation.

According to the findings of neuropsychology, however, both hemispheres of the brain are involved in hypnotic or suggestive procedures. In the left hemisphere, the analytical and critical part of the brain, where the language center is also located, the suggestive instructions must be linguistically prepared, that is, formulated. These commands then migrate to the right hemisphere, the "holistic" or holistically oriented part of the brain, where this suggestive process is further intensified and lived out through feelings and visual images, and only upon completion of this step does it unfold its full suggestive or hypnotic effect.

Therefore, it is not surprising that autosuggestive approaches are often used to induce relaxation, as in autogenic training. At the same time, this method is applied in so-called "mental training," which, for example, adopts "positive thinking" or other fantasy or imagination exercises through suggestive self-commands and is accompanied and supported by corresponding (positive) mental images or pictures.

Since no person can be hypnotized against their will, it can be assumed that the willingness for hypnosis or self-suggestion presupposes a certain degree of self-confidence and emotional stability. Anxious individuals would be reluctant to self-hypnotize or to surrender to a foreign person as a hypnotist and would likely react reservedly to hypnosis and probably reject it.

2.3.2 Manipulations of Other Target Persons

Just as well as a person can influence themselves, he or she can also demonstrate and apply the talent for suggestion or systematic influence towards others or external persons. However, these classic manipulations are characterized by their secrecy and disguise, because only *covert* manipulation attempts are manipulations in the true sense of the word. Thus, these deliberately conducted manipulations are about specific tangible advantage calculations and not about the defense against negative and threatening attacks, as was meant by the reaction of "deceive, camouflage, and hide" (see Sect. 2.2.3). To influence or direct someone, something is preferably "slipped in" to him or her, cleverly packaged in ambiguous, ambivalent hints or messages.

All activities aimed at putting another person into a certain state of mind (e.g., into a cheerful mood or supposed well-being) to then more easily begin the actual influence maneuvers and assert one's own interests also fall under the construct of "suggestiveness" to achieve "suggestibility."

Individuals find it difficult to "harness" others for their own selfish motives and systematically influence them to their own advantage if they cannot do so due to their naivety or their imperfect personal charisma, for example, because they fail to flatter with compliments or the like, or to charm or ensnare others, and thus never succeeded from their own experience. Or it is far from them for ethical-moral reasons to influence other people in such a way and to take and rob them of their free will.

In psychology, the "Machiavellian" corresponds exactly to the unscrupulous type of (secretive and cunning) manipulator who ruthlessly uses systematic influence for their own advantage, even at the expense of disadvantages to other persons (see also Sect. 4.1.2.4).

2.4 Lies and Other (Supposed) False Statements

Essentially, lying is either about systematically influencing the questioner, whose specific questions the respondent tries to evade with evasive or false answers, or about the conscious intention of the "liar" to feign something and avoid the revelation of the truth for selfish reasons at all costs. But since lying can have different degrees of manifestation and can also take on different qualities depending on the situation, it makes sense to treat and discuss it as an independent construct.

2.4.1 Witness Statements Do Not Necessarily Correspond to the Truth

For criminologists and lawyers, the interrogation of witnesses is often associated with false statements due to erroneous observations, false memories, or incorrect conclusions. It is a different matter when a witness consciously tells an untruth, that is, in the truest sense of the word, lies (see next section 2.4.2). More likely is the "distortion of the truth" expected from suspects or defendants who simply want to "save their necks or get out of the noose" and aim for the prosecution to present solid evidence. Sometimes a judge in court proceedings is then forced to demand and order statements under oath.

According to the findings of court experts or specialists, a statement under oath is a delicate matter, as false statements are punishable as perjury. This applies not only to defendants but also to unsuspected witnesses, who then expose themselves to the accusation of "obstructing justice." In many cases, this deters witnesses or suspects from insisting on their previous (false) statement, but instead, they correct it or weaken it by relativizing *"It could have been different – I'm not so sure anymore"*.

Witnesses are not forced during interrogations to accurately reproduce everything they have perceived, but they should indicate if the memory of the observation might be uncertain so that the criminal investigator can adjust to it during the interrogation and record it correctly as a statement.

Moreover, witnesses are expected to later reproduce or repeat exactly what they said and testified to the criminal police during the interrogation in court proceedings (possibly under oath).

2.4.2 Lies

When it comes to the topic of lies, so-called half-truths must first be differentiated from actual lies spoken with full intent. *Half-truths* are fundamentally omissions, where things are deliberately concealed or very "twisted" in the sense of being downplayed or reported tendentiously, mostly to "lead the listener or conversation partner astray." In contrast to blatant lies, they contain a, albeit often more or less insignificant, portion of truth or "true core." Furthermore, they are limited to directly answering the posed question and omit all other information or observations that would further illuminate and clarify the situation.

Similar, yet different, are white lies. These are particularly used by suspects under stress to get out of a tight spot with false statements and "to give themselves some breathing room" or to divert attention from themselves. If they are later proven to have made a false statement, they resort to excuses or apologies, such as *"But I understood it differently back then!"*, and try to rectify the situation for themselves afterward.

Real lies are thus conscious and blatant false statements that are repeatedly repeated and confirmed upon inquiry against better knowledge. This also includes denying or disputing facts or events in response to specifically posed questions, such as *"Were you at the crime scene at that time? – Yes or No?"*. Liars are thus concerned with the conscious and intentional staging of a story that is untrue or fictitious but perhaps plausible, which they maintain and defend under all circumstances until proven otherwise.

A special form of lying or systematic influence is "feigning false facts," as lawyers call it when they speak of false and untruthful claims that serve deception. From a psychological perspective, feigning false facts is a problem of "fiction and truth" (see Chap. 5)! In a milder form, self-presentations could fall under this, which are associated with the so-called "impression management." This also includes the deliberately created questionable or false impression when someone wants to "adorn themselves with borrowed plumes," as well as the simulation of a certain psychological state, such as a (feigned) illness or disorder.

People who acknowledge personal responsibility for events or for fellow human beings certainly do not come into the temptation to lie. They stand by their word and their statements, even if it is difficult for them and brings noticeable disadvantages or negative consequences for them.

2.5 Summary

Apparently, the presented scheme as a matrix or "four-field table" helps to gain even more clarity in the discussion about manipulative behavior. Thus, some forms and manifestations of manipulation maneuvers could be distinguished, which may be helpful for psychodiagnostic purposes. Consequently, lying has a different quality than, for example, deceiving or disguising to pretend to be stupid and

2.5 Summary

ignorant. Voyeuristic behavior, understood as a craving for sensation and sensationalism, seems to differentiate itself from self-influence (autosuggestion) due to the lack of self- or impulse control. The remaining sub-constructs or facets of manipulation, which were already present in the cited system for manipulation, could also be classified and integrated into this system as a matrix.

Behavioral Manifestations of Manipulation

3

Finding behavioral descriptions of manipulation attempts should not be particularly difficult. The "item universe" of manipulative behavior could be enormous and possibly even "limitless," as manipulators constantly come up with something new in their imagination to influence their fellow humans in their favor. However, as became clear from the constructs or facets of manipulation (see Chap. 2), with the exception of autosuggestion, this interactive game always involves two actors: one who manipulates and another who allows themselves to be manipulated—and possibly does not even notice or realize it.

In the already mentioned work "Manipulation as a System" (Wienkamp, 2022a), there are already two behavioral examples for each of the five more closely described mechanisms or sub-constructs of manipulation for illustration. Building on this, further behavioral manifestations could be identified, collected, and specified, which, however, follow the adapted and new systematics here with *seven* manipulation characteristics. All listed behaviors are in all probability content-valid or have a "face validity."

In addition, the rule was adhered to and practiced as a procedure to combine and list both active and intentional manipulation attempts as well as more passive or preventable influencing actions.

The collected behavioral descriptions or episodes of manipulation are listed in the following Tables 3.1, 3.2, 3.3, 3.4, 3.5, 3.6, and 3.7.

3.1 Behavior Descriptions of Suggestivity

Following the logic, manipulation can only succeed and occur if there is a person who practices manipulative behavior and tries to apply it secretly or covertly to others. In other words, this person must have the gift or predisposition of influence

Tab. 3.1 Suggestiveness

Item No.	Polarity	Item
1	+	It is important to place ideas or suggestions in such a way that the other person thinks or feels they came up with them themselves.
2	+	I enjoy leaving others in the dark; the more willingly they will follow my suggestions.
3	+	I believe that I can put the right or appropriate words in others' mouths.
4	+	It is better to speak in images or examples than to use linguistic-logical arguments.
5	+	To be effective, I would rather rely on moods and feelings than on logical reasoning.
6	+	Flattery or compliments are helpful in reducing reservations or resistance.
7	+	I like to give others a "push."
8	+	Many people are influenced or captivated by hearing what they already knew or what is familiar to them.
9	+	I can immediately assess people, what they can do for me or whether they are useful to me.
10	+	By initially signaling agreement to the other party, it becomes easier for me to counter.
11	+	Sometimes it is advantageous to only hint at things and consciously offer room for choice or interpretation.
12	+	I feel that others observe me very closely, how I behave.
13	+	When I talk to others, I feel they listen to me attentively.
14	+	Many cannot resist the need to constantly observe me.
15	–	When people put on airs, it exposes them.
16	–	I find it difficult to reprimand others.

and behave skillfully in its execution to avoid being discovered in their manipulation attempts and attracting negative attention. However, a gift or talent for skillful execution of hypnosis is not required. Furthermore, manipulators must have no scruples about applying their influence techniques and using them to their own advantage, even if their "victims" suffer disadvantages and, which should not be underestimated, are deprived of their freedom of will.

In addition, there are related attributes for behavioral manipulation, such as persuading a person to do something or the somewhat more elegant expression "convincing." Sometimes, certain character traits or attitudes can already make an impression on other people and influence behavior, such as constant criticism or showing off.

Behaviors or items with positive polarity (+) signal an active role in influencing other people, while a negative polarity (−) suggests a certain restraint or a negative attitude towards the ability to influence.

3.2 Behavior Descriptions of Suggestibility

Tab. 3.2 Suggestibility

Item No.	Polarity	Item
1	+	If others find out what opinion I hold, I would advocate for it even more and propagate it enthusiastically.
2	+	I am receptive to moods.
3	+	I am pleased when I find confirming evidence for my assumptions or speculations.
4	+	I gladly take up a salesperson's sales arguments, as they help me justify a purchase both to myself and to others.
5	+	Fear can create a reality that one has feared.
6	+	If I had failed my last exam, I would automatically withdraw from an already agreed employment out of shame.
7	+	When I order a meal in a restaurant, I always follow the waiter's recommendation.
8	+	If several of my neighbors have hired the same gardener or craftsman in the past, I would join them if needed, without much thought.
9	+	If I see that two buyers purchase the same item from a given selection, I know what I would buy if I had the choice.
10	+	Many people only look for confirmations when forming their opinions and easily overlook contradictions.
11	−	Even if a good friend or acquaintance had given my name as a recommendation, I would still not buy something at the door.
12	−	My carefreeness is immediately over when I realize that someone wants to influence me quietly and secretly.
13	−	When I notice that someone is trying to slip something to me or insinuate something, I immediately become suspicious and refuse to play along.
14	−	The path of least resistance is not always the best.

3.2 Behavior Descriptions of Suggestibility

Even though no one can be hypnotized against their will, there are individual differences in susceptibility and dependence on the influence attempts of others. A tendency towards susceptibility can occur unconsciously and spontaneously, but it can also be consciously and sometimes gratefully received. As already indicated, the motives for being influenced by others are quite diverse and sometimes, for example, desired for reasons of convenience. Convenience may be an important reason or motive for the occurrence of susceptibility. Additionally, other inclinations or human weaknesses may promote suggestibility, such as the weakness of "taking everything at face value," that is, believing carelessly and accepting it as reality without questioning it (see also Sect. 3.6).

People who are reluctant to be told anything and initially react negatively to all well-intentioned advice are also not "easy-care" companions and, due to their

Tab. 3.3 Autosuggestion

Item No.	Polarity	Item
1	+	When I imagine something intensely, I feel a corresponding sensation somewhere in my body.
2	+	I live for my ideals and pursue them intensely.
3	+	Sometimes it helps a person to say to themselves, "it could have been much worse."
4	+	When things aren't going well, it's nice to let oneself fall back a bit and dream of nicer, better things.
5	+	When I have made a difficult decision, I become increasingly convinced of my choice over time.
6	+	My gut feeling tells me whether I am right in a decision or action.
7	+	When someone acts stupidly towards me and I can punish them for it, it gives me a nice feeling of satisfaction.
8	+	Sometimes it's just like that, when I see that someone else is worse off, I feel better.
9	+	A failure, mishap, or defeat is never something final for me, but only something temporary.
10	–	When I feel like I know someone well, I start to doubt.
11	–	I am rather a self-critical person.
12	–	Many people suffer from not being able to control their flow of thoughts or ideas and being temporarily overwhelmed by it.
13	–	I find it difficult to turn my imagination into action.
14	–	Whoever always thinks of the worst is deluding themselves.
15	–	By acknowledging negative conditions that have occurred, one gains distance.

resistance to advice, are generally difficult and indeed "not easy-care." On the other hand, there are also behavioral traits that strictly oppose any form of influence, provided the person to be influenced becomes aware of the manipulation and regards it as an attempt to influence.

Under certain circumstances, distrust, risk aversion, or a certain skepticism may be at play, triggering and accompanying the exhibited behaviors.

3.3 Behavior Descriptions for Autosuggestions

Individuals who have the talent to easily influence themselves have it fundamentally easier in life. They are not only in a better mood but usually also manage to believe in themselves and realize what they have set out to do. Autosuggestion can also be a prerequisite for not only influencing oneself but also convincing oneself!

3.4 Behavior Descriptions for Camouflage, Deception, and Hiding

Tab. 3.4 Camouflage, Deception, and Hiding

Item No.	Polarity	Item
1	+	I would prefer to suppress a true statement in favor of another, but not correct statement, to create a better impression.
2	+	Concealing something is less bad than lying.
3	+	If I feel that everyone or many are against me, I "give in," even if it is not the case.
4	+	It is not difficult for me to say something about everything.
5	+	If I am invited to a job interview, I would make an intense effort to make a good impression, even if the behavior shown does not correspond to my true nature.
6	+	I believe one must shed many tears to be believed.
7	+	With conscious flattery, otherwise unavoidable conflicts can be circumvented.
8	+	I prefer to talk about challenges rather than problems.
9	+	Some people are often forced to pretend because their environment only wants to see what it wants to see.
10	+	Maintaining the facade is particularly important to many.
11	+	I prefer to say "Yes, but …" rather than a clear "No," even though I think so.
12	+	If I have not understood a question correctly, I prefer to answer it with "Yes," even if that might be wrong.
13	−	I would assume that if someone shines through pronounced ignorance, they are putting on an act.
14	−	If a witness avoids chronological sequences or changing locations, it is a sign that something is wrong.
15	−	As soon as someone has a "false smile" on their face, do not believe them.
16	−	People who pretend or (supposedly) show remorse often have something up their sleeve.
17	−	Before I say something wrong, I prefer to leave it out.

People who avoid self-influence either let themselves drift or shield themselves from emotional reactions or the like, or, figuratively speaking, acquire an "armor" that everything bounces off.

3.4 Behavior Descriptions for Camouflage, Deception, and Hiding

Seemingly out of a human weakness, individuals tend to unconsciously "make themselves small" to reveal as little as possible about themselves. They either pretend to be dumb and ignorant or juggle with half-truths or let essential information "fall under the table" to lead others astray.

Tab. 3.5 Lies

Item No.	Polarity	Item
1	+	It is not difficult for me to make unproven claims.
2	+	I believe it is not difficult to attack someone and later portray oneself as the victim.
3	+	Even a false claim will eventually be believed if repeated constantly.
4	+	It seems to be true that people do not mind being deceived as long as they do not notice it.
5	+	When asked about prohibited behavior, I resort to excuses or deny it.
6	+	I would never tell a person that I wish them to take on a task or job—although I secretly wish it.
7	+	It would not be difficult for me to assume different identities and deceive others.
8	+	Someone who tells the truth under oath can also lie on another occasion.
9	+	By omitting or leaving out certain events, deliberately false or misleading impressions can be provoked.
10	−	Lies can be exposed if the accounts show only moderate coherence and lack any peculiarities or noticeable features.
11	−	I would definitely avoid unproven claims.
12	−	When I see someone anchoring their feet around the chair legs, I know something is wrong or probably not true.
13	−	When someone wrinkles their nose, they apparently do not feel comfortable in their skin.
14	−	It would not bother me to admit embarrassing incidents or events like losing a driver's license, failing exams, etc.

It cannot be said that these "deceivers" are particularly cunning and skillful; rather, their "false" behavior is dictated by necessity. Unlike lying, such individuals experience these embarrassing situations as an emergency, which they can only escape through these rather unconscious reactions.

3.5 Behavior Descriptions for Lying

Apart from so-called "white lies," which can occur spontaneously and unintentionally from a defensive stance, deliberate conscious lying is a blatant misconduct that, upon discovery or exposure, is likely to lead to a massive breach of trust and loss of reputation.

As can be seen from the following behaviors, there are different "varieties" of dealing with the truth in an unlawful and morally highly questionable manner. Lies "not only have short legs," as a saying goes, but also many faces!

3.6 Behavior Descriptions for Prejudices or Stereotypes

Tab. 3.6 Prejudices or Stereotypes

Item No.	Polarity	Item
1	+	I would mostly assume events based on "hearsay" to be true and not question them, because they actually could not have happened otherwise.
2	+	Many people find it easier to form a judgment when a suspect has already committed the offense in the past.
3	+	The reputation or image of a person has a decisive significance for me in important decisions (e.g., when choosing a partner or babysitter).
4	+	I can well imagine that certain medications develop or intensify symptoms of illness, which only lead to a disease after their intake.
5	+	Those who are rich or very wealthy should not be surprised if their home is broken into more frequently.
6	+	If there is a risk that an item could be rationed or become scarce, I would secure a larger supply as a precaution.
7	+	I hold firmly to my principles.
8	+	Someone who does not believe in miracles is not a realist.
9	+	Whoever always assumes the most negative outcome can never be disappointed.
10	+	I share the view "opportunity makes the thief" and consider all temptations to be questionable.
11	+	There is some truth to it, if you give someone an inch, they will take a mile.
12	+	Some people always have to make a mountain out of a molehill.
13	–	I can well understand that those who behave badly or poorly do not necessarily have to be bad or evil.
14	–	Idols have never held great significance for me.

3.6 Behavior Descriptions for Prejudices or Stereotypes

Those who nurture their prejudices often make life easy and comfortable for themselves and are self-sufficient. Another form of prejudice or stereotype could be gullibility, which is actually a sign of a dependency relationship and prevents the formation of one's own opinion, as it is also more convenient and comfortable to join another's preconceived opinion.

Prejudices or stereotypes are sometimes applied unconsciously and simply slip into these individuals' thinking and judgment processes.

Tab. 3.7 Voyeurism

Item No.	Polarity	Item
1	+	Reading crime novels is interesting and exciting because someone else "gets their hands dirty" and takes over solving the case.
2	+	If I happened to be present at a serious accident, I would definitely try to take photos with my phone.
3	+	I like to watch people who don't mind, for example, riding a roller coaster or exposing themselves to other intense thrills.
4	+	When two people are having an animated conversation, I absolutely have to listen in (eavesdrop).
5	+	When two people are arguing, I can't help but watch the event until the end.
6	+	If I had binoculars, I would use them without scruples for (covert) observation of other people.
7	+	I find TV reality shows like "Jungle Camp" or "Big Brother" exciting and don't want to miss them.
8	+	I am absolutely in favor of filming the behavior of unsuspecting people with video cameras in appropriate places.
9	–	I believe "stalkers" live in a parallel world when they fight for something they never had.
10	–	People who take photos of accident victims and post them online cannot be helped.
11	–	I don't necessarily have to be present at a bank robbery.
12	–	People who make very personal photos or views public are foreign to me because it repels me.

3.7 Behavior Descriptions for Voyeurism

Voyeurism has already been sufficiently discussed in the context of the influence of psychological processes (see Sect. 2.1.2). The crucial point here is that affected individuals enter into a psychological dependency, similar to an addiction or vice. Voyeurs find it impossible to resist temptation in the relevant and significant situations. Generally speaking, their behavior is impertinent, namely shameless and scandalous. Sometimes voyeurs are found in an active role when they, for example, actively observe other people; in other situations, they delight in what others are doing. Voyeurism, as well as stalking, is considered irrational behavior because the affected individuals cannot escape their urge or vice. Whether their behavior already exhibits delusional traits is debatable. A well-known forensic psychiatrist provides a very convincing and accurate definition, originating from one of her colleagues, for madness and to clarify it: "Madness is building your own castle in the air and living in it" (Adshead & Horne, 2022, p. 346). Perhaps these characters also live in their own castle in the air, without necessarily being aware of it!

3.8 Summary

Models or constructs are one thing, but the concretizations of these characteristics and their operationalization for practice are another. From the "universe of behavior patterns," with some thought and mental imagery, it is certainly possible to find meaningful behavior examples, as is common in the construction of psychological tests.

For the *seven* sub-constructs of manipulation discussed here, it was possible to find sufficient behavioral manifestations that would provide a good platform for the further development and construction of suitable psychodiagnostic procedures.

Differential Diagnostic Aspects of Manipulative Behavior

In a differential diagnostic consideration of a psychological model or construct, two essential aspects must be observed. Firstly, this psychological characteristic, or the associated sub-constructs or feature facets, must clearly distinguish and differentiate itself from other (not similar, thus unrelated) personality traits. Secondly, it is important and generally to be expected that individuals also differ individually in the expression or intensity of this personality disposition if they belong to different characters.

Similar or related personality traits may have content overlaps or correlative connections that need to be empirically statistically determined and demonstrated. Personality researchers would then speak of *convergent* construct validity. The case would be exactly the opposite if there were assumptions or hypotheses highlighting significant or diametrical differences between absolutely dissimilar or different traits, as would be expected with *discriminant* construct validity.

4.1 Construct Validity of the Trait Manipulation

For the investigation of construct validity, it is important on the one hand that the feature facets belonging to this personality trait correlate highly with each other in some way, if this is required and appropriate in terms of content, such as between the sub-feature "Deceiving-Concealing-Hiding" (see Sect. 3.4) and the sub-feature "Lying" (see Sect. 3.5). On the other hand, assumptions or hypotheses about content connections (or non-connections, e.g., as so-called "zero correlations") to other traits not necessarily equated with manipulation, such as neuroticism or conscientiousness, are to be formed or excluded and empirically verified.

4.1.1 Connections within the Trait Manipulation between the Defined Feature Facets

Perhaps it makes things easier if, for the defined feature aspects of manipulation, a look is taken at the listed and formulated behaviors as items of these "sub-traits" (see previous Chap. 3). At least, alongside the fundamental mechanisms and orientations of these sub-constructs in the construction of this personality trait of manipulation (see chapter 2), there are sufficient behavioral examples available in concrete form.

The simplest and most promising approach seems to be the one between a presumably active role on the one hand (see Table 4.1—active or "Attack") and a passive role on the other hand (such as passive or "Defense"). We can also say that active behavior is goal-oriented, while a more passive behavior contains a degree of restraint or endurance. Seen in this way, the following facets or sub-features of manipulation would covary with each other and aim in the same direction.

Active behavior in this context means, on the one hand, a certain degree of self- or behavior control, and on the other hand, taking situational risks. In passive behavior, control over the current situation and one's reactions to it is likely lacking. People who see themselves in this role and behave accordingly are usually overwhelmed by either their emotions or the events and are unable to escape them. It can also happen with individual sub-features that both behavioral qualities appear alternately (e.g., in voyeurism), but according to the chosen classification, one quality is either likely more dominant or simply situation-dependent.

With this division, it is assumed or suspected that the sub-features with the same orientation correlate more strongly with each other, as the same disposition or tendency is effective behind them. In contrast, when comparing active vs. passive behavioral directions of manipulation, it is expected that they either reveal non-correlative relationships or even show negative correlation relationships, as would normally be expected, for example, with suggestiveness as influencing ability and suggestibility as susceptibility to influence.

If these correlations occur as assumed, then the construct of manipulation would have both inherent convergent and discriminant construct validities, and this would substantiate the construct validity in content.

Table 4.1 Differentiation of feature facets according to active (= Attack) or passive function (= Defense)

No.	Feature Facet	Active	Passive
1	Suggestiveness	X	
2	Suggestibility		X
3	Autosuggestion	X	
4	Deceiving-Camouflaging-Hiding		X
5	Lying	X	
6	Prejudices or Stereotypes		X
7	Voyeurism	(X)	(X)

4.1 Construct Validity of the Trait Manipulation

From the so-called "central traits" (see e.g., Gatewood & Feild, 1987, p. 438), the dimension "Activity" with its manifestations "active vs. passive" was already applied a priori for supplementary validity testing, albeit for obvious reasons without statistical findings and evidence. To what extent the other two dimensions "Value" and "Power" can contribute to a central, i.e., overarching variance explanation, is left to later empirical research.

4.1.2 Connections to Other Personality Traits or Test Scales

Elsewhere, one or another indication has already emerged that certain personality traits, such as Machiavellianism or curiosity, are closely related to certain aspects of manipulation and certainly have overlaps. It is certainly necessary to examine and discuss the question of the tendency to influence or susceptibility to influence with the long-standing findings on personality development, such as "emotional stability" or the fundamental orientation towards extraversion on the one hand and introversion on the other.

Recently, personality research has also extensively dealt with the rather not very human-friendly personality types of the "Dark Triad" (see Sect. 4.1.2.4), which are known to possess a high and deterrent potential for manipulation.

It is not by chance that in earlier times it was customary to install an additional lie scale alongside the personality variables and to make the interpretation of the test results dependent on the overall score in the lie scale.

4.1.2.1 Connections to general "classical" personality traits

As soon as it comes to the analysis of personality, we cannot avoid the basic structures of personality development. Preceding and decisively shaping further personnel research, such as the development of the "Big Five," was Eysenck's personality model (1970) with the constructs (see also Fig. 4.1): *Extraversion-Introversion, Neuroticism* and *Psychoticism*. Extraverts are outward-oriented and inclined towards other people, while introverts are inward-directed, thus more focused on themselves. Lability, nervousness, and a general insecurity or anxiety are symptoms of neuroticism, and psychoticism is closely related to psychopathic and psychiatric abnormalities, i.e., abnormal behavior patterns, and can be briefly described as maladaptive social behavior, regardless of which category it originates from. For Eysenck (1981), people with high psychoticism scores have a "Super Ego" and are therefore likely to possess a high degree of manipulative ability and to use this potential unscrupulously if it helps and benefits them. Their behavior can take on both aggressive and parasitic traits.

While Eysenck, based on the collected test results and the factor expressions previously determined after a factor analysis (these are the high or low loadings of the test statements or items), still found somewhat reliable and interpretable personality profiles for dysthymic abnormalities (these are psychiatric syndromes caused by anxiety, such as obsessive-compulsive disorders), the forms of hysteria

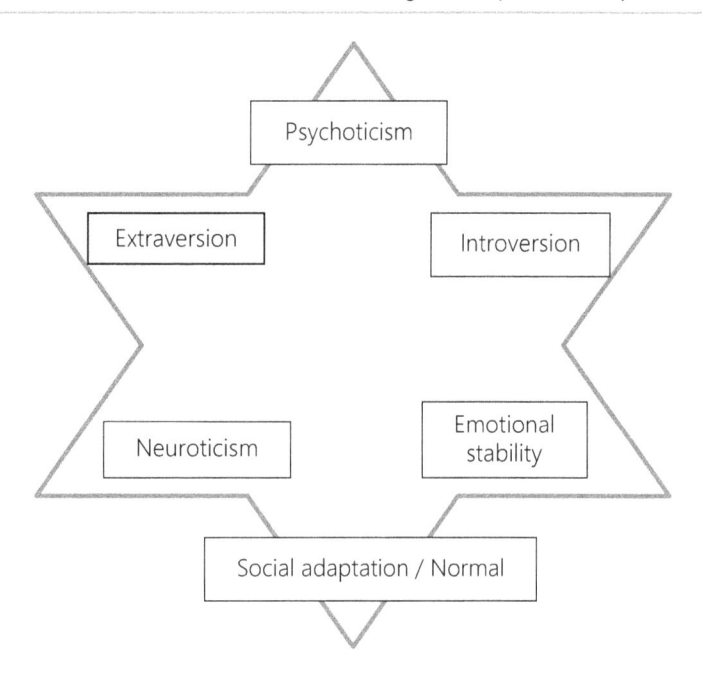

Fig. 4.1 The personality model: $E - N - P$ by Eysenck (in own representation)

could not be depicted "spotlessly" in his model, so over time his research efforts turned more towards antisocial psychotic behavior (cf. Gray, 1981).

According to the experimental findings already available at that time, introverted people are much more "conditionable," i.e., influenceable, than inconspicuous individuals and certainly more so than extraverts. For Eysenck (1977), introverted individuals perceive critical situations simply with more seriousness and caution, which protects them from maladaptive social behavior. The situation is completely different for extraverts, who were harder to condition in the experiments and cared less about rules or commands. This statement was supported by a study cited by Eysenck (1981, p. 19) by Tranel (1961) with extraverts and introverts on enduring perceptual isolation by the instruction to remain "completely still" for an indefinite period. Surprisingly, the extraverts tolerated this situation better because they simply ignored the instruction and self-stimulated during the experiment, which the introverts did not do and strictly adhered to the rules.

In the context of manipulation chosen here, introverts are therefore likely to be more easily manipulated due to their conditionability than other individuals who do not possess this personality trait. However, there were also situations in which extraverted individuals showed particular appreciation for social rewards and attentions ("Social Rewards") and were more strongly impressed by them (see Wilson, 1981, p. 218).

4.1.2.2 Connections to the "Big Five" Constructs

Of the "Big Five" traits: (1) Neuroticism, (2) Extraversion-Introversion, (3) Conscientiousness, (4) Openness to Experience, and (5) Agreeableness, certainly not all behavioral or personality dispositions are equally associated with manipulations.

Easily influenced individuals might exhibit a disposition towards lability and thus emotional instability, which would tend towards neuroticism. Regarding the remaining "Big Five" constructs (Costa & McCrae, 1992; McCrae & Costa, 1999), no immediate content overlaps with influenceability are apparent. Eysenck (e.g., 1970 and 1977) mentioned, however, that introverted people not only condition better and faster but are also more likely to develop and effectively use a "conscience"—and thus experience guilt, which determines behavior either a priori or the state of mind afterward, i.e., ex post.

All behavioral tendencies that lean towards deceiving, disguising, or even lying are psychopathic as well as sociopathic tendencies that are ostracized in a social community and should not occur. These detrimental behavioral traits should therefore negatively correlate with the "Agreeableness" construct from the Big Five.

In the *HEXACO* variable (Lee & Ashton, 2004) *"Honesty – Humility"*, "liars" would certainly perform poorly and, if they complete the test truthfully, achieve a low score. Thus, a negative correlation would also be expected in the result.

4.1.2.3 Connections to Emotion-Focused Models and Self-Influencing Factors

Those who can easily influence themselves must have a good mental imagination and enjoy using imaginations or images. Furthermore, in such a context, an optimistic type inclined towards positive moods is more likely to be expected than a pessimistic type, so that the tendency towards autosuggestion could be associated with *wishful thinking* (possibly also openness to new experiences).

Autosuggestive and self-influencing factors are, in addition to personality disposition, highly dependent on the *situation*. The situational component refers to the triggers for a given natural tendency towards spontaneous, subconscious reactions, which closely interact with personality development and manifest in *impulsive* behavior, but also in *anxiety-laden* reactions. Despite the expansion of Eysenck's "classic" personality model (the E – N – P; see Fig. 4.1) by the model of the "Big Five" enriched with additional personality traits, personality psychology as a whole found it relatively difficult to make modifications to Eysenck's model that would change the basic structure.

Even with the question posed to personality research and its models in general, which Gray (1981) subjected to Eysenck's personality model in the form of an inventory and critical analysis, namely not only to ask: "Does it work?, but what's it for?", to infer from the aspect of descriptive behavior descriptions to the underlying behavior-causing motives and reasons, new insights and impulses emerged for research.

Without fundamentally questioning the basic structure of Eysenck's personality model, Gray (1981) came to the realization that a number of existing research findings could be better explained and interpreted if the personality dimensions of Extraversion-Introversion on the one hand and Neuroticism (vs. emotional stability) on the other hand were connected by the diagonals *anxiety* and *impulsivity* as sub-constructs, and their behavioral intensity depended on different levels of arousal and not on thresholds that block behavior (figuratively speaking, the two axes, namely Extraversion-Introversion and Neuroticism, would be rotated by 45°). It is also plausible that these two driving forces, anxiety vs. impulsivity, correspond with each other reciprocally, so that with increasing impulsivity, anxiety decreases (and vice versa), which is often observed in psychopaths.

According to Gray's new personality model (1970, 1971, 1987) and the later revised version of the "Reinforcement-Sensitivity-Theory (RST)" by Gray and McNaughton (2000), fear is associated with a sensitivity to punishments and avoidance behavior, as punishments, etc., must be avoided or circumvented at all costs, and impulsivity is associated with a sensitivity to rewards or other incentives, which are to be pursued and achieved through approach behavior, in whatever form. Based on these centers for sensations and supported by new neuroanatomical and neurophysiological findings, Gray hypothesized that there is a "Behavioral-Inhibition-System (BIS)," a "Behavioral-Approach-System (BAS)," and a "local site" in the central nervous system, the "Fight-Flight-Freeze-System (F-F-F-S)," which is causally responsible for panic attacks and phobias. On the basis of these neuropsychological systems, Gray developed his "Reinforcement-Sensitivity-Theory" as a possible alternative to the already established and known other personality theories.

It should also be mentioned from experimental research that introverts and extroverts depend on the time of day in their reactions, for example. Introverts are more awake and perform better in the morning, but are slower and more tired in their reaction ability in the evening; for extroverts, it is exactly the opposite. Gray (1981, p. 258) suggested that the findings obtained for Eysenck's personality model might depend on the time of day and seriously question their general validity!

It would be advantageous that this model modification would allow some experimental findings to be explained more plausibly as well as the correlations (or factor loadings) of statements or items in the associated trait scales. For example, it would be plausible if items of the trait *impulsivity* correlated positively and approximately equally with both neuroticism and extraversion.

Recent research activities have led to the conclusion that when using psychometric investigation methods such as psychological tests or trait scales, it is best and most skillful to start from a construct of *"incentive motivation"* and *"risk propensity"* with the poles *risk-taking* or *sensation seeking* and *risk aversion*, in order to interpret the results obtained from surveys as best and plausibly as possible (see Wienkamp, 2017, 2020a). Incentive motivation, in particular, has a high potential for manipulation due to the enormous self-interest, to achieve self-serving (selfish) goals. As a representative of many antisocial and possibly criminal behaviors, reference is made to cheating in exams or fraudulently obtaining social benefits from the "public purse," insurance fraud, and tax evasion. In short or summed up, incentive motivation can be described as *instrumental* behavior as follows: *"To do something in order to get something"* (Wienkamp, 2017, p. 9). But risk behavior also only manifests when appropriate situational incentives are present, so that taking risks is worthwhile at all (even if only to avoid boredom).

Sensation seeking, as a significant "driving force" or behavioral impulse of voyeurism, is a character weakness that is most likely accompanied and supported by involuntary impulsivity in behavior. This is also evident in the lack of *self-control* (in tempting situations) and *empathy* for the people who find themselves in the victim role against voyeurs or even stalkers. As far as is known, there are currently no standardized diagnostic procedures for determining voyeuristic tendencies.

4.1.2.4 Connections to the so-called "Dark Triad"

Machiavellians, as a representative of the personality types of the Dark Triad (see Jones & Paulhus, 2014), are, for example, masters in influencing other people and in the application of subtle influence techniques, so that the people exposed to manipulation often do not even realize that they are being secretly manipulated. Thus, a close connection between these constructs of suggestibility on the one hand and Machiavellianism on the other would be expected and demanded.

In this context, psychopathological behavioral tendencies are also particularly relevant as another "pillar" of the Dark Triad, which stand out and are to be criticized due to the demanding and ruthless claims against the given interests of a social community.

Narcissists, as the third type of the Dark Triad, manipulate their social environment for entirely different motives. They want to be noticed and admired or even loved in an enhanced form at all times. If they do not receive the desired attention and recognition, they become angry and abusive, by no means are they satisfied with the status quo. It is also conceivable that narcissists tend to lie or deceive, as all means are acceptable to them for their personal well-being, which they use unscrupulously to gain recognition.

4.1.2.5 Personality Tests with a Lie Scale

With the onset of psychological diagnostics based on personality tests and trait scales, the capture of lies or dishonest, untruthful answers was already considered, which are either labeled as a *"Lie Scale"* or a *"Social Desirability Scale"*. A prominent and early representative of this category was or is the test *"Minnesota Multiphasic Personality Inventory (MMPI)"* by Hathaway and McKinley (1943/1951), which was later adapted to German conditions and published in German (Spreen, 1963). The Lie Scale contains a total of 15 queries, which are simply answered with *"yes"* or *"no"* (as are all other scales of the MMPI), such as *"I do not always tell the truth"* or *"I do not like everyone I know"*, etc. In German, there are different versions of the MMPI, one with the original 566 items and after revision to the MMPI-2, a version with 567 items (see, for example, an online published variant with 567 statements: "The MMPI Test Questions:

All 567 True/False Questions" at https://psychtest.de/mmpi-test-questions). Thus, there may be slight linguistic deviations (or nuances) in individual items of the Lie Scale. Another version provides an example of this and contains, for instance, the item *"I do not like every of my acquaintances"* (https://career-test.de/einstellungstest/minnesota-multiphasic).

A negative answer to the lie queries is an indicator of lies or untruths or "Social Desirability" in all versions, although from a moral standpoint, the "no" answer would have been the "better" but not the more realistic answer, and can, if occurring frequently, impair and question the entire test result. For Spreen (1963, p. 24), high L or lie values indicate an above-average stubbornness and low insight. Furthermore, higher L values are said to correlate with psychopathological and paranoid behavioral traits.

Hathaway and Meehl (1954, p. 290) themselves state that standardized L values of this Lie Scale of 70 and above should be treated with utmost caution, as the test results are very likely to show invalid, i.e., embellished answers.

It should be considered and taken into account when evaluating the MMPI scales that a conversion of raw scores into T-scores occurs according to the formula: T-score $= 50 + 10 \; (X - MW_x) / SD$ (see, for example, Spreen, 1963, p. 19), where MW is the average or mean value of the population group and SD represents the standard deviation. Thus, this expression is at the same time the so-called "Z-score" of a normal distribution, expressed in standard deviations or probability statements. A T-score of over 70, for example, indicates that its occurrence in the population group is to be expected with a frequency or probability of no more than 3%.

Whether the critical opinion about the MMPI or MMPI-2 regarding the construction and application by Hank and Schwenkmezger (2003), presented as a test review, also refers to the Lie Scale of this personality test, was not discernible from the statements. However, this critical appreciation also met with serious opposition and was massively "torn apart" by Engel (2003) in his subsequent reply.

When discussing the diagnostics of psychiatric syndromes or constructs, as with the MMPI with its diverse traits like psychopathy, paranoia, etc., and that still in connection with a lie scale implemented in the test, the "classic" personality test "EPQ" by Eysenck and Eysenck (see, for example, 1991) with the constructs of extraversion, neuroticism, and psychoticism (see Sect. 4.1.2.1) should not remain unmentioned and omitted. Eysenck and Eysenck also had the Lie Scale processed in their test to control the answers, for example, with the item *"Have you ever lied in your life?"*. The interpretation of findings from test participants with high psychoticism scores and *simultaneously* high scores on the Lie Scale could be difficult and lead to a *paradox*. High Lie Scale scores signal caution against hasty conclusions from the test results, as the subject tends to "put themselves in a good light," which relativizes the result and may appear questionable and not very credible. On the other hand, individuals with psychotic behavioral traits have no scruples about telling untruths, so lying is normal for them, which would explain the higher scale values on the Lie Scale. Admittedly, it is not easy to escape this tautology and break the circle or cycle of contradictory test findings and "make sense" of this result.

Ruch (1999) already noted in a study on the revised German version of the EPQ the close relationship of items on the Lie Scale to the Psychoticism Scale. After a factor analysis, for example, the item *"Do you always insist on having your own way?"* loaded not only highly on the Lie Scale but also highly on the Psychoticism or P-Scale.

4.1.2.6 Connections to Prejudices or Stereotypes

In the past, positive correlations have already been found in social psychological surveys between the habit or attitude of preferentially using prejudices or stereotypes in personal evaluations and the tendency towards *dogmatism* or also *authoritarianism*. Perhaps a *limited capacity for thinking* also favors the recourse to prejudices and stereotypes, which should also be reflected in the correlation relationships.

Starting with the research work of Adorno and colleagues on a systematic survey and investigation of fascist and authoritarian tendencies, which among other things ended with the construction of the so-called *"F-scale"*(see Adorno et al., 1950) as an instrument and led to worldwide popularity after the end of World War II, Rokeach (1960) occupied a similar research terrain with his *Dogmatism Scale ("D-scale")*. However, dogmatism corresponds more to the notion of "conventional narrow-mindedness" (see Wienkamp, 2022a, p. 28), narrow-mindedness, and rigidity, if one follows Rokeach, and covers more the type of thinking of a person sympathetic to ideology and deals less with the specific contents of this ideology. In a nutshell, it can be claimed that dogmatists pursue their firm "convictions" and are not quickly willing to put them up for discussion. Later research findings were also able to demonstrate that highly dogmatic individuals held on to their prejudices more strongly and were guided by them in their judgment formation, but there were no connections to tendentious political attitudes, such as right-wing extremism.

New developments in this type of feature scales as survey instruments can also be identified and are widespread in the German-speaking area. For example, the scale *"Motivation for Prejudice-Free Behavior"* (Banse & Gawronski, 2003) aims at diagnosing precisely not applied prejudices, which were captured with the sub-scales (1) "Behavioral Control," (2) "Admitting Own Prejudices," and (3) "Prejudice-Free Self-Presentation" towards foreigners (here Turks) and homosexuals, which emerged through the comparison of implicitly and explicitly obtained attitudes. According to the test's prediction, high scale values are less likely to be associated with a discriminatory *explicit* attitude, while the implicit attitude remained unaffected and did not change.

4.1.3 Bizarre Types According to the Observations of Theophrastus

When people think of peculiar or strange characters, they certainly automatically think of the ancient Greek philosopher named Theophrastus (see, for example, the editions by Rüdiger, 1949; Steinmann, 2000; Klose, 2000 and Plankl, 2014). All 30 characters of Theophrastus are given different names or labels in the cited publications, but they each refer to the same type of person in content. For instance, one speaks of the "master of disguise," who is referred to in another work as the "deceitful" or "insincere" person. Of the 30 Theophrastus character portraits, some characters could be relevant in terms of manipulation. Admittedly, in the selection made here, the behavior descriptions or anecdotes indeed show concrete attempts at influence or deception in the sense understood here, while this is at most less obvious in the remaining characters, as their behaviors regarding influences are more subtle and less clear.

4.1.3.1 The Insincere
Thus, the insincere or deceitful person is a "master of self-diminishment," who is reluctant to "show his hand" and as a witness never noticed or saw anything or could not remember it (Rüdiger, 1949). Such a type of person tends to feign a false reality and certainly masters the art of deception and disguise. He likes to deliberately "mislead" other people or influence them in their perception and situational judgment.

4.1.3.2 The Rumormonger
The rumormonger invents stories that he likes to tell others "in confidence" exclusively. Or as it is stated elsewhere: "Rumormongering is a construction of untrue reports and events that are meant to be believed according to the will of the rumormonger,…" (Steinmann, 2000, p. 41). These invented and constructed stories are usually based on "hearsay," and the alleged sources are equally fabricated. To critical questions like "Do you really believe that?" he responds with the remark that this news will soon spread, and everyone will know it then. But at that moment, the rumormonger makes his conversation partner a secret bearer and deliberately and intentionally his accomplice.

4.1.3.3 The Braggart and Fame-Seeker
Braggarts and fame-seekers, also called "fibbers" (Steinmann, 2000, pp. 72 f.) or "boasters" (Rüdiger, 1949, pp. 54 ff.), are not very particular about the truth. They strive to "throw dust in the eyes" of others and deliberately deceive them. They are not far from outright lying, although it should be noted that they do not intend to harm or disadvantage others. They just want to make themselves interesting and gain recognition and satisfaction in this way. For example, a "braggart" is said to have told a visitor, as a tenant of an apartment, according to Theophrastus, that he inherited this apartment from his father and is likely to sell it at a good price now—which, of course, was not true.

4.1.4 Noticeable Strange Characters in Our Time

New strange types of people also appear in our present time due to observations, as Ortheil (2022) has described and caricatured, for example. Finally, it must be noted that the repertoire of strange manipulative personalities is possibly inexhaustible! Here is initially a "sample" from Ortheil's collection.

4.1.4.1 The Embellisher
For Ortheil (2022, pp. 48 f.), the embellisher is a person who "lives in a fantastic world to which only she herself has access." In her imagination, she invents stories or legends that sound nice and that she embellishes, but unfortunately do not correspond to reality or facts. Embellishment is thus nothing other than deceiving oneself *and others*. Or, as Ortheil (2022, p. 48) puts it: "In truth, her world consists of stories that she (herself) could have experienced or would like to experience."

4.1.4.2 The Hasty
The hasty are always ahead of things or the future. As Ortheil (2022, p. 105) has formulated, they "always have the next possible thing in mind." In doing so, they influence events, whether they are situational events or people. For example, it is the hasty who immediately call for a second checkout to be opened when there is a queue at the supermarket, thus "taking command." The cashiers or employees of the store then have to "dance to their tune"—immediately and without objection. This is nothing other than social influence.

4.1.5 And are there more "odd birds"?

Perhaps in the aforementioned reading, one or another peculiar and unnamed personality was simply and plainly forgotten or omitted. However, this should not be a reason to overlook and not consider them. The following characters might still "cross our path" in one situation or another or try to influence us.

4.1.5.1 The Hypocrite
In my opinion, the list by Ortheil (2022) is missing the "Hypocrite," who is also commonly known as a deceiver, Pharisee, or even a liar. A hypocrite is sneaky and deliberately deceives others by pretending to be something he or she is not; or acts as if and then behaves differently. It is also said that hypocrites preach to others to drink water while they themselves enjoy wine, or in other words, others should be moderate and frugal while they secretly indulge and live it up—possibly at the expense of others! In short, hypocrites live by their "own" rules and enjoy themselves in the process.

In their piety, hypocrites, hence the term, do not like to be outdone by others. Thus, hypocrites like to point to their religiosity and emphasize their special moral standards for themselves, which later turns out to be pure hypocrisy, as illustrated by the aforementioned examples of behavior as expressions of "parasitism or sponging."

The attempts at manipulation by hypocrites lie in the formation of impressions and deception of their true character, which observers should not adopt.

4.1.5.2 The Know-it-all

Know-it-all behavior is extremely annoying and unpleasant for the affected and suffering fellow humans. Know-it-alls should not complain that they are either avoided or ignored in their attempts to lecture. Often they think they not only know everything better and "have a monopoly on wisdom," but they must "add their two cents" to everything. But their "smart-aleckness" is rather superficial and lacks depth. True to the motto "Big talk, and nothing behind it"! When it comes down to it, and they are confronted by skeptics or critics, they have little to offer besides nice words or empty phrases, which is revealing for all involved.

Perhaps somewhat less intrusive, but equally "nerve-wracking" are "windbags," who do not necessarily claim to know everything better but must comment on everything with meaningless words to try to impress others.

4.1.5.3 The Worrywart

Also not particularly pleasant to deal with are the so-called "worrywarts," who can neither decide nor motivate themselves to do anything. With their constant concerns, they block events and ongoing processes and are a "hindrance" to their social environment.

Comparable, but not entirely identical, are worrywarts with the "Yes, but types," who constantly question everything (Ortheil, 2022, p. 15 f. called them "The But-Sayer"). Yes, but types also cannot decide on something or an alternative; they tend to automatic reflexive counter-reactions with their "Yes, but," no matter what is proposed.

Worrywarts, on the other hand, see everything negatively and become fixated on what doesn't work or isn't possible. Naturally, they also find it easy to deal with partly unjustified criticism, whether about people, processes, or situations.

4.2 Connections to "objective" measures as a sign of criterion validity

People with a pronounced ability to influence are likely to be more successful in certain professions than others who do not possess this gift or talent. Everyone certainly thinks of sales representatives, who as sellers must convince their customers of their offered products if they want to succeed and make a living. The criterion for "salespeople" would thus be the sales or sales revenues.

But entirely different professional fields must also use suggestiveness as a "tool and art" when it comes to shaping other people entrusted to them, whether in sports through appropriate training or in school during lessons and learning in general. Essentially, every consultation contains a minimum level of influence if it is to be effective and successful. The success criterion would then be the successful implementation of these consulting activities or suggestions, which is reflected in the learning or training successes, such as in competition by receiving a winner's medal, of the target persons in need of advice.

On the other hand, people such as students must also be willing to be advised and to listen to something, and to accept help or advice if they want to succeed in the end. In other words: They must show a willingness to be positively influenced.

Self-hypnosis or autosuggestions are shown, for example, in the speed and intensity of achieving physical relaxation, which, however, can only be reliably determined through neurophysiological recordings.

Neurophysiological measurements also occur during lie detector tests to measure the stress or tension that liars or people with false statements feel at the moment. According to the available findings, in more than 80% of cases, a false claim or statement can be proven as a lie based on the recording protocols (see e.g., Schauer, 2022, p. 121 and Sects. 7.3.1.2 and 8.3).

Whether there are also objective criteria or concrete situational circumstances in the occurrence of voyeurs or stalkers is probably a speculative question. It rather seems that random events, such as a serious traffic accident, allow voyeurs to get their money's worth by taking photos with their cell phones or standing out as "rubberneckers."

Prejudices or stereotypes as "guidelines" in evaluations or decisions are probably only ascertainable and recordable through observations and experiences.

4.3 Summary

Without a validity check, the research and construction of personality traits remain "halfway" and would be incomplete. Both construct validity and, if suitable criteria are available, criterion validity should be empirically demonstrated through correlation relationships as measures of connection. Moreover, construct validity is also supported if there are demonstrably reliable relationships to other personality traits as well as to known personality types, which either share a common core or differ from each other as expected. All validity checks ultimately depend on the quality and measurement suitability of the instruments and systems used as trait scales.

To round off the discussion on construct validity, the characters of Theophrastus from antiquity and the peculiar personality types from modern times, which could be associated with manipulative behavioral traits, should not be forgotten.

In earlier years, there have often been attempts in test development to either implement so-called "validity scales" such as the lie scale into the test or to develop suitable test scales separately for certain constructs (e.g., by using and employing "inverse items" with negative statements that may need to be negated).

Individual Diagnostics: Distinguishing Between Fiction and Truth

Starting from the many possibilities previously outlined for dealing with reality in both positive and negative ways, verbally (or even non-verbally), for example, by distorting facts or denying the truth, thus by unconsciously or consciously "misleading" or lying with full intent, the question then arises of how to proceed in communication with other people or parties with opposing interests. Many professional roles, which also have the task of mastering investigations or interviews, and these are not only criminal investigators or judges in court, but also managers or personnel managers, etc., are constantly striving not to be deceived and to find out the truth. Such conversation or interview partners can also be involved in disputes or conflicts and must give a hearing to both the target person, e.g., as a complainant, and other involved persons (e.g., as defendants or neutral witnesses). For personnel matters, this initial situation for the necessary investigations or interviews could be represented as follows (see Fig. 5.1).

As can be seen from this diagram as a systematics for interviews, both the perspective and the type of information to be expected are different and may require a differentiated methodology in the approach. It is clear that complainants, due to their own involvement, describe the process very subjectively. Other people who have observed the event from a more neutral position contribute "second-hand information" from a greater distance or rely on so-called "hearsay," which may again be what others thought they observed or heard. If even both aspects of this "secondary analysis" apply, the problem of *fiction* and *truth!* becomes all the more apparent.

Methodologically, it depends on the "spoken word" of the participants and interviewees, which must be carefully documented and played back in every conversation. Other methods, such as psychological tests, whether with or without a lie scale, generally do not come into consideration and use.

© The Author(s), under exclusive license to Springer-Verlag GmbH, DE, part of Springer Nature 2025
H. Wienkamp, *Diagnostics of Manipulations*,
https://doi.org/10.1007/978-3-662-70435-6_5

What is the problem?

No.	Criterion	Affected party	Other persons
1	Perspective	Own point of view	External perception
2	Type of information	Self-awareness and experiences	Observations as 2nd hand information
3	Diagnostics • Methodology • Special Challenges	Problem analysis + Distinguishing between fiction and truth + Recognize understatements/ exaggerations	Secondary analysis + Check consistency + Make comparisons
4	Result • Shape • Indication	Problem sketch/scenario as feedback e.g. coaching or therapy	"Plausi - Check" e.g. change to an assessment
5	Practical examples	Complaints or work disorders	Conflicts in appraisals Decision after the probationary period

Fig. 5.1 What is the problem? (from Wienkamp, 2023b)

5.1 Statements of an Affected Person

Understandably, everyone tries to make themselves heard who is currently suffering from a problem or conflict for which they hold other parties responsible. In the workplace, for example, employees go to their supervisor or boss when they get into a dispute with a colleague and the collaboration is disrupted. Or they turn to the human resources department if they have problems with their direct supervisor, for example, because the last employee evaluation was unexpectedly poor, which they perceive as unfair and incomprehensible. Many evaluation procedures have therefore provided institutionalized conflict resolutions and are usually documented and adopted in company agreements to deal with these problems or disputes in practice (see, for example, Wienkamp, 2022b).

Institutionalized conflict mechanisms provide, for example, in the case of differing opinions between the parties about an employee evaluation, that with the involvement of the *next higher* supervisor, i.e., the supervisor of the evaluator at the next higher management level, the human resources department, and possibly the works or staff council, if it is the employee's wish, the points of contention are addressed. In a similar formation, other issues in organizations are also discussed and addressed.

When involving the personnel department, the responsible personnel officer first conducts a confidential "one-on-one" conversation with the affected employee as the target person or, for example, as the complainant. In doing so, the affected person presents their subjective "view of things." From a methodological perspective, this is a *problem analysis* for the human resources representative, which corresponds more to an inventory, initially without evaluation and judgment, and where it is merely about obtaining the *complete* picture from the perspective of the affected employee to do justice to their concern. At most, the personnel officer asks questions for understanding or follow-up questions to draw a meaningful *problem sketch*, which they then play back to the employee at the end of the conversation (or conversation chain) as feedback on their statements and have them confirm. From the conversations conducted, the representative of the human resources department tries to secretly recognize, for example, attempts at dramatization as exaggeration or the downplaying of unfavorable events as understatement and to differentiate between "fiction and truth" from this (and possibly other implausibilities).

The interviewer should be particularly sensitive to whether the respondent is addressing or meaning the actual and correct problem at all or whether there is a problem shift. It is well known that management literature (Drucker, 2009, p. 26) has already earnestly pointed out that incorrect or inappropriate solutions for the right or relevant problem are easier and more readily corrected than correct solutions for the wrong problems. If, for example, an employee complains about disruptions in the team or in collaboration with colleagues, it does not necessarily have to be due to a lack of team building or "team spirit," but it can also be due to a personality disorder or crisis of the affected person themselves (e.g., due to inferiority complexes as the "actual problem"), which they are keen to suppress or disguise. These unacknowledged personality problems force the person to defend and repress the issue.

It is important in this problem analysis to refrain from making any kind of judgments and also not to give any hidden non-verbal or verbal signals of agreement or skepticism. It may not always be easy for those responsible for personnel to remain neutral and objective and not be impressed or influenced by the statements. That in the end, there is also the indication that further discussions according to company regulations or prevailing practices with the other side or with other parties involved, e.g., as witnesses, are necessary, is probably self-explanatory.

5.2 Statements of Other Persons as Participants

As in legal proceedings or matters, after the presentation of problem descriptions or accusations by those affected, further inquiries may be necessary. Thus, further discussions are to be conducted both with the opposing party as the cause, injurer, or accused, as well as with neutral observers of the event as witnesses or similar. According to this interpretation, these are external perceptions or observations that do not necessarily have to correspond to the perspective of the affected target person in the role of the plaintiff. Since these are observations or experiences from another perspective, it is permissible at this point to speak of "second-hand information" either from the accused opponent or from uninvolved third parties.

Conceptually, therefore, a distinction should be made between the problem analysis of the affected person as a methodology and procedure and the *secondary analysis* based on statements and observations from other persons, whether directly involved or neutral.

5.2.1 Statements of the Accused (as "Opponent")

In whatever context accusations occur, the accused or defendant must, in any case, be questioned for reasons of fairness, to give him or her the opportunity to present his or her perspective as a counterstatement.

Even in the conversation with the affected person as the complainant, it could not be ruled out that false claims or facts were presented. This danger or situation applies even more to the interrogation of suspects. Tendencies to falsify or even blatant lying to "save one's own skin" is a fact that criminal investigators deal with every day (see also Sect. 10.3.3.1).

But not only lies are to be expected; during interrogations or similar, one must also reckon with covert attempts at influence for one's own benefit and to create an impression on the conversation partners, which can take manifold forms. Not without reason, in addition to lying or deliberate false statements, attention was drawn to cunning approaches or behavioral maneuvers, particularly "deceiving, camouflaging, and hiding" (see Sect. 3.4), which involve the deliberate omission of important information or facts or so-called "half-truths," and which are meant as an independent behavioral trait of manipulation.

Against this background, the sub-constructs of suggestibility and lying, in connection with their possible behavioral manifestations (see Chap. 3), are to be taken very seriously. Perhaps these behaviors can contribute important clues regarding the search for truth in the relevant interrogations or send signals that suggest and justify a particularly critical attitude towards the statements made.

5.2.2 Statements of Uninvolved Persons or Witnesses

It can be assumed with goodwill that neutral observers have no interest in deliberately producing false statements and possibly exposing themselves to the risk of later prosecution precisely because of false statements or "obstruction of justice" or the ongoing proceedings. Nevertheless, it can happen that the descriptions do not or not entirely correspond to the truth and are not "objectively correct." Memory gaps, false perceptions, and especially misattributions or erroneous or superficial conclusions of the observed event can occur and happen at any time during witness interrogations.

Whether, for example, prejudices or stereotypes against certain groups such as foreigners, disabled people, etc., might also impair and affect one's own judgment is furthermore a major problem with the statements of witnesses and the subsequent assessment and search for truth. For example, in earlier times, Sinti and Roma, as "nomadic contemporaries," lived with the prejudice of sedentary residents that they tend to steal (a discriminatory saying was, for example: "When the Z. come, you must take down the laundry."). Thus, these tendencies to falsify also encompass and envelop the already mentioned problem of "fiction and truth"—now viewed from a different perspective.

Besides the possible influence of prejudices or the like, some witnesses are also susceptible to other influences, especially when the interrogation, for whatever reason, is very unpleasant for them, and they are reluctant to make a statement at all. Reluctance is, in any case, a reason to avoid answering uncomfortable questions. In not a few cases, they then just want to get the interrogation over with quickly and agree to what the interrogator or questioner wants to hear or "puts in their mouth," which they then affirm. This does not even have to mean the use of leading questions.

According to the experiences of court experts for witness statements or interrogation specialists, it seems particularly important that the event is carefully and precisely reconstructed and that the witness cannot get away with superficial statements. For example, the chronological sequence or the exact order at changing locations is an important criterion for the credibility of the witness statement (see Sect. 10.3.3.2). It is not without reason that it is customary and sensible to record witness interrogations and have them confirmed by signature.

5.3 Reactions of Onlookers and Voyeurs

The gawking, as preferred and practiced by onlookers and voyeurs, appears repulsive and by no means worthy of imitation to many people. Surveys on motives for voyeuristic behavior only come about when, for example, criminal charges are filed because the sensation-seeking spectators, for instance, blocked the way for rescue workers or the police and hindered them in their work, which also led to untimely, delayed assistance and, in the worst case, fatalities. Whether anything can be made of the respondents' answers remains to be seen! It is more likely to expect appeasements, denial of the underlying motives (such as sensationalism), and "crude" excuses.

Let us also remember the television images when onlookers refused to follow the instructions of the authorities because they did not want to be deprived of their "personal pleasure" from "cell phone snapshots."

Behaviors of onlookers and the like can be captured either through on-site observations or through recordings such as by cameras.

5.4 Summary

In the individual diagnostics of affected and uninvolved persons, such as witnesses, outlined and described here, it is important to remain objective and neutral and not to be influenced or even deceived. For effective conversation management, sensitivity to problem shifts or their suppression is also required.

Various methods are available to the conversation leaders. In particular, it is important and actually a matter of course to record statements in writing and to continuously provide feedback to the conversation partners until the "picture" is fully drawn or the actual problems and their causes are known and undisputed.

6 Manipulation by System

Manipulations are most easily carried out through generally binding regulatory systems. A prominent example is traffic regulations. Strategic considerations that serve one's own advantage in the preparation and planning of an event or process are more required in social interactions, such as in the conduct of games, which also have a set of rules, like chess, but additionally allow and leave many potential courses of action to the involved players.

6.1 Orders and Regulations

Manipulations can, which may be surprising at first glance, occur through a system or through its system rules themselves. Many people are not even aware, or they accept it as a given natural order, when they are influenced by an existing system with its instructions or regulations, or better, when their behavior is controlled for the general well-being and benefit of all involved. The best example, as already mentioned, is traffic rules, whose non-compliance either leads to disasters in the form of serious accidents or to traffic fines—or even to both. Everyone knows the traffic rule: "Right before left" or the generally valid order "Right-hand or left-hand traffic." How dangerous a violation, especially against the right-hand traffic applicable to us, can be observed and understood from the so-called "wrong-way drivers" on the highway, who not only put themselves but also the oncoming traffic in mortal danger.

6.2 Games and Their Strategic Calculations

To behave in accordance with the law in road traffic, strategic thinking and action are generally not required and also not necessary, as might be the case in other circumstances. Similarly, strategic reasoning is not required in "one-man games" or when a person plays against nature, as Binmore (2009, p. 25) expressed it. A nice example is the situation of a farmer who considers whether, based on today's weather forecast, he can dare to harvest or bring in the harvest? He is then playing a game against nature, or as happened here, with the weather. This situation is comparable to a walker who faces the decision of whether to take an umbrella or not? In such situations, people seem to be making a "bet with themselves"!

Strategic thinking in the form of successful planning of moves, on the other hand, characterizes actors whose decisions and behavior are in a mutual dependency relationship and the associated intentions and preferences. As is well known, a game always involves two parties who play against each other, i.e., interact, and each wants to win, which the opposing party wants to prevent in its own interest and thwart with its moves and counter-reactions, either resulting in a draw or as its own victory or success of the game.

The science or methodological concept for strategic thinking or behavior in game situations was provided by the eponymous game theory. Game theory only works on the assumption of the rationality of the participants, who try to make the best possible moves for themselves and are consistent in their decisions. The most illustrative examples are chess, poker, but also auctions, whose outcome also depends on the expectations and bids of the interested parties present and participating.

To avoid misunderstandings, rational thinking and action do not mean predicting the event in advance, but knowing and determining the alternatives for action and their benefits in order to be able to assess the possible consequences and results based on them. Irrational thinking, as sometimes occurs with otherworldly romantics or "crazy" people, does not meet the norm or concept of rationality when no comprehensible decision criteria exist and everything depends more or less on chance or the current mood. The concept of game theory is based on the selection of the best possible own decisions and moves by both players, who pursue the same intentions.

6.2.1 Elements of Games

Games not only have rules in the sense of binding instructions or limits, but "the salt in the soup" are their success or winning strategies, which are particularly preferred and skillfully applied by experienced players. From more conceptual or methodical-analytical aspects, there are also models that reveal something like regularities for one game or another, which favor faster or more advantageous solutions if they are known and considered by the players. A solution concept for an analytical rational game strategy would be the "Nash Equilibrium," which would be a "best-practice strategy" for both players or parties, as there is no better or more successful action strategy as an alternative.

The Nash Equilibrium is applied in both pure game strategies and mixed strategies.

6.2.1.1 Nash Equilibrium

An "analysis tool" developed for games is the Nash equilibrium, which offers both players a way to find the best or optimal decision based on their respective expected and calculated benefits, taking into account the given risk due to the possible self-interested moves of the opposing party.

A Nash equilibrium thus arises when both parties simultaneously and independently make the "best" decision or response for them in reaction to the expected decision of the fellow player. The decision is not only the most advantageous reaction for both players or for one of the players who has a so-called "dominant strategy" (see Sect. 6.2.1.2), but also without alternative!

For some game configurations, there is indeed the possibility of achieving an even higher joint benefit, but this would require cooperation, which is not given in simultaneous non-cooperative games under competitive conditions, and on the other hand, none of the players would expose themselves to the risk of a major disadvantage or failure because the other player has reconsidered and does not cooperate, but rather "cold-bloodedly" and unscrupulously takes advantage of the potential benefit offered. Just as well, the other player can make a different decision spontaneously or purely by chance, so to speak "for the fun of it," and thus behave unpredictably or irrationally. This risk problem is particularly impressively expressed in the game "Prisoner's Dilemma" (see Sect. 6.2.2.1).

Nash equilibria are often circular or tautological in nature when the players' considerations revolve around how one player thinks about the other (and vice versa), resulting in an endless thought process about the possible moves of the respective other party. Best examples of these speculations are constellations where one wins everything and the other loses everything and vice versa, which would mean two Nash equilibria, and additionally a constellation that is balanced from a risk perspective and would be acceptable for both sides, leading to another Nash equilibrium. Just as multiple Nash equilibria can occur in a game, there are also games, like the zero-sum game "Matching Pennies," also known as the coin toss "Heads or Tails," that do not exhibit a Nash equilibrium (see also Sect. 6.2.2.1).

In the following exemplary game types, the reference and the special impact of a Nash equilibrium on the pending decisions or moves will be further deepened and illustrated. Besides the game type, the identification of Nash equilibria primarily depends on the duration or initial situation of the game and the given strategy form.

6.2.1.2 Strategy Forms and Moves

Games can be played as *"pure"* or *"absolutely"*, i.e., without probability expectations and with *100 percent certainty* of a chosen move, thus with complete or "perfect" information as a *pure strategy*, or as *mixed strategies* with assumed probabilities for the alternative moves in question depending on personal preferences as utility or payoff.

Depending on the expected results, usually represented using a "payoff matrix," the choice, if possible, is to play a *strictly dominant strategy*, as specified in Fig. 6.1 as a pattern, where, for example, a specific decision of one player (here player A with move 1—new investments) is preferred over the other alternative moves of the player (A) regardless of the reactions of the fellow player (B), as it is consistently better or more advantageous according to the expected payoffs (the utility would be "3" and "5" in this example). The disadvantaged opponent (B) then chooses the decision alternative that brings him the greatest benefit. In the terminology of game theory, the strategic decision options or moves of this fellow player (B) are *strictly dominated* by player (A) and thus "suboptimal" or "inferior."

It should be noted in passing that the gains or losses in the payoff matrices are in many cases less exact quantitative calculations or computations, but rather a *qualitative preference structure* of the involved persons in the form of a ranking or ordinal scale or simple (direct) assessments that attempt to realistically depict the held notions.

The content of Fig. 6.1 can be interpreted as follows:

"The actors A and B face the decision to either leave everything as it is or to intensify and expand their business activities, whether through additional investments in product development, market processing, or in work processes, for example, through more digitization.

However, the initial situation of these two companies is different. Company A would definitely benefit from additional investments, regardless of how competitor B behaves, and would have a dominant strategy (associated with a Nash equilibrium). Thus, the strategy "new investments" is almost obvious for player A.

Competitor B, unfortunately, is not in such a comfortable starting position. On the one hand, it would very likely lose the competition in light of A's new investments and waste unnecessary resources (therefore the utility or payoff is 0), on the other hand, it can only hope that A's new investments do not meet A's cherished claims, so that its strategy to maintain the status quo and conserve its available resources is the best solution for it. Additionally, there is the prospect of possibly copying and imitating A's successful innovations later. Therefore, this constellation is also advantageous for B due to the associated flexibility (hence payoff = 2), as if everything in the market remains as it is, which is expressed by the status quo of both market participants and would also bring a benefit of 2 to market participant B.

That competitor A refrains from new investments for incomprehensible reasons and possibly lets competitor B take the lead seems illusory in view of the lower utility values."

Player: A (rows) / B (columns)	New investments	Maintaining the status quo
New investments	0 3	2 5
Maintaining the status quo	3 1	2 2

Fig. 6.1 Payoff matrix with strictly dominant strategy of a player (A)

In complex games with more action alternatives than moves, the aim is to eliminate strictly dominated decisions or moves, as they logically do not have a Nash equilibrium and only contain and exhibit the worst results (see the example of Dixit & Nalebuff, 1995, p. 72, about the simulated deployment of hits of planned offensive weapons, e.g., drones or missiles, and the possible defense of the opposing side with alternative defense systems from the Iraq war of the Americans, which led to the elimination of the least effective, i.e., dominated, formations).

Strategies should also be oriented towards the given initial situation or game setup. Game theory distinguishes in this context between simultaneous and sequential games. *Simultaneous games* are usually non-cooperative games often with only one upcoming move (such as the "Prisoner's Dilemma" game; see Sect. 6.2.2.1). Strategy decisions in this game are usually made independently by the actors, separately and without the possibility of agreements. In their considerations, the involved players should orient themselves towards the existing and recognized Nash equilibria and use them as a measure of their decision.

In contrast, *sequential strategies* can have both a certain (final) number of moves and be played infinitely often ("repetitively"). One player starts and makes the first move, which the other player acknowledges and responds to according to their considerations or preferences. In the next subsequent move, the player who started first is up again and chooses their response based on the known decision of the opponent. Such a game with repeated moves can, if you will, go on endlessly. However, the present players are expected and required as "good strategists" to mentally play through the possible moves of both parties to the end (or as far as possible) and to know or calculate the chain of moves with the resulting payoff values as results. Starting from the payoff matrix available as the final result, they should then go back or trace back and reconsider their respective first move or "put it to the test" and decide on the best or most promising opening move. In the English-speaking world, this game setup is referred to as "Backward strategy" or *"Backward induction"* (see e.g., Binmore, 2007, p. 37 ff.). A *decision tree* as a tool or instrument can be a valuable help to the participants.

Some "player natures," detached from the strategic considerations and dispositions within the framework of game theory, still have rather "idiosyncratic" playing styles, which could possibly also lead to success, but appear rather unconventional and arbitrary. For example, an established company could constantly search and observe the market for innovations from, for example, new "start-ups" and, in case of market success, copy these products or imitate these innovations (see Dixit & Nalebuff, 1995, p. 15) or it could simply buy out the start-ups with their know-how or participate in the company.

Another playing style would be to simply rely on chance, such as choosing the color *Red* at roulette and then at some point choosing the color *Black* again, to pursue a so-called *"randomized strategy"*. In interactive games, this approach creates a high degree of unpredictability for the fellow player, as they have no clues about what and when something will happen to them. As will be shown, there are also games, especially the "win or lose games" or also called "zero-sum games," where it depends on chance and how to deal with random events in order not to act irrationally.

6.2.2 Selected Popular Game Types

Of the many conceivable games, some are very popular and have already become "classics," such as the game "Prisoner's Dilemma." Nevertheless, it makes sense to roughly categorize the many games, such as into "non-cooperative games" and "cooperative games," to gain (and maintain) an overview of the "universe of games."

Non-cooperative games are characterized by a, as already indicated, *simultaneous* decision situation and usually have only *one* move, so that no revenge or retaliation by the fellow player or the opposing side for "suffered grievances" is possible afterward. In contrast, cooperative games can either be played finitely with a defined number of rounds or, in the extreme case, repeated indefinitely. Due to the possibility of continuing to play, both parties ideally have an interest in cooperating, as the opposing party can retaliate in the next round for any unfair play experienced. Ultimately, this attitude results in a tacit agreement or "division of labor."

6.2.2.1 Non-cooperative Games

Games that aim solely at winning or losing cannot be inherently cooperative but rather pay homage to the competition among players. In its purest form, they are "zero-sum games," such as in the toss of a coin with heads and tails. Either the one who chose heads wins if heads appear, or otherwise, the one who favored tails wins. Alternatively, two coins can be used, where it is then about either *matching* symbols, i.e., heads: heads or tails: tails, or *non-matching* symbols. In English, this is referred to as "Matching Pennies," for which the payoff matrix in Fig. 6.2 applies (see, for example, Binmore, 2007, p. 10).

If we add the values in the aforementioned cells of the matrix, we always get zero as a result, hence the name "zero-sum game." The probability for a game configuration (e.g., heads: heads) is 0.25 or 25% each. Thus, each player (A or B) has

Player: A (rows) / B (columns)	Head	Number
Head	- 1 + 1	+ 1 - 1
Number	+ 1 - 1	- 1 + 1

Fig. 6.2 Payoff matrix for the game with two coins and heads or tails

the chance to win—or lose—with a probability of 0.25 + 0.25 = 0.50 or 50% in each game round. The best strategy for each player would be the (mixed) strategy, namely to maintain their once-made decision, such as heads: heads, over all game moves, as a better starting position or probability than 50% as a total result over potentially infinitely many games is not to be expected. With a random-dependent (randomized) strategy that includes alternating decisions, a worse overall result may be expected. Games like "Matching Pennies" fundamentally have no Nash equilibrium (see Osborne, 2004, p. 29). In a mixed strategy with a chosen fixed probability by both players, even zero-sum games, like all other games, have a Nash equilibrium if both players, for example, operate with a probability of 0.5 (see Binmore, 2009, p. 169).

Another well-known game is the so-called "Chicken Game," which is also designed for victory or defeat. It differs from the "coin toss" game in that both players want and must avoid a certain game outcome that could end in disaster, such as a serious accident. According to the well-known film version "Rebel Without a Cause" starring James Dean, it is a car race with only two possible actions: either continue at full speed ("Speed") to win or dodge the competing vehicle and possibly stop and safely lose. Represented as a payoff matrix, this results in the image shown in Fig. 6.3.

It is easy to recognize that if both drivers continue to race at unabated speed, a "crash," that is, an inevitable serious accident, must occur if the racetrack has bottlenecks or narrow sections that only allow space for one vehicle. In this respect, neither player would gain anything, and the supposed benefit would be negative (−1:−1). On the other hand, whoever yields to the other driver and lets them go first has lost, so the benefit is zero, while the other emerges as the winner (benefit = +3). However, if both, so to speak, "cooperate" and swerve or drive slower, the benefit would be equally high at +2 for both "racers," as they have a common interest in avoiding an accident. This constellation or game outcome would then be the actual Nash equilibrium, as continuing to drive would indeed yield a higher benefit in a victory, but in this game, the fellow player can prevent this by behaving equally selfishly and essentially irrationally. According to game theory, however, this strategy would also lead to a Nash equilibrium with a possible benefit of

Player: A (rows) / B (columns)	Dodge, stop	Continue driving (speed)
Dodge, stop	+2 +2	+3 0
Continue driving (speed)	0 +3	-1 -1

Fig. 6.3 Payoff matrix for the "Chicken Game"

+3 mutually for each player or one player (see Binmore, 2007, p. 14). For other authors (e.g., Holler & Klose-Ullmann, 2007, p. 48), there is no Nash equilibrium in the Chicken game, as each player could improve their individual benefit through the action "Speed"—but certainly at the cost or rather with the risk of an accident, which would be an irrational reaction and would contradict the necessarily assumed principle of rationality.

Similar to the previous Chicken game, the "Prisoner's Dilemma" game also has several Nash equilibria, which, however, differ in their benefit and are either secure or insecure for the players as suspects. In the Prisoner's Dilemma game, the "Crown Witness Rule" applicable in the USA, combined with immunity in the case of a confession and incrimination of an accomplice or partner, likely set an impulse. This game was then able to establish itself for many applications both in practice and in experimental social research.

The following dramaturgy is foreseen for this game (see Fig. 6.4):

"1) Two suspects are caught after committing a crime and interrogated separately. Communication or collusion between the defendants is not possible and is fundamentally excluded.
2) Both suspects are separately offered the Crown Witness Rule with the note that if they confess and incriminate their accomplice, and the other accomplice does not confess, they will receive *immunity* for this offense. The accused accomplice then receives the *maximum sentence* after indictment and conviction.—In some game versions, confessing defendants were charged with another less serious offense and received a minor penalty (e.g., in the case of a serious armed robbery as the main offense, a mild penalty for illegal possession of weapons), which perhaps was even suspended on probation.
3) If both confess, they are indicted and receive a reduction in sentence of a few years, so that a *medium* punishment as a penalty is to be expected.
4) If both prisoners *do not* confess, they cannot be convicted, so they may only be charged and punished for another legal violation (e.g., for speeding before being apprehended by the police). Overall, in this case, the penalty is likely to be rather *mild*."

According to the available research findings, the majority of test subjects confessed in the first round to "play it safe." Over time and after several rounds of the game, participants in the experiment learned and cooperation occurred without prior agreement, i.e., both players did *not* confess and thus maximized the total benefit, resulting in $2 + 2 = 4$ according to the payoff matrix, instead of $1 + 1 = 2$ or $3 + 0 = 3$ (cf. Binmore, 2007, p. 80 ff.).

With the possibility of playing multiple, i.e., repetitive rounds, the prisoner's game gradually transitions into a cooperative game.

6.2.2.2 Cooperative Games

As already indicated, cooperative games are based on multiple rounds, which open up the possibility of accommodating the fellow player through cooperative play

6.2 Games and Their Strategic Calculations

Player: **A** (rows) / **B** (columns)	Confession	No confession
Confession	+1 Medium sentence (e.g. 5 years) +1	0 Impunity and maximum penalty (e.g. 10 years) +3
No confession	+3 Impunity and maximum penalty (e.g. 10 years) 0	+2 Mild penalty (e.g. 1 year) +2

Fig. 6.4 Payoff matrix in the Prisoner's Dilemma game

and rewarding them or taking revenge and punishing them in the next move in the case of unfair play, i.e., deception or cheating. In this way, both players can influence each other through threat and deterrence. Especially in cooperative games, the command or principle of reciprocity and thus rationality applies.

Two versions are fundamentally distinguished in cooperative games: On one hand, a game, such as the Prisoner's Dilemma, can be played multiple times or even endlessly, with each new round being its own game. Cooperation or retaliation occurs when the other player has behaved cooperatively or non-cooperatively in the previous move. Such games are played based on *social reciprocity*, or *"Tit for Tat"* (see also Sect. 9.1), which means nothing other than "How you treat me, so I treat you" or: "An eye for an eye, a tooth for a tooth"! With a cooperative style of play, both sides achieve their Nash equilibrium, i.e., the maximum benefit. In common parlance, it is also said: *"You meet twice in life."*

Reciprocity is also inherent in everyday life when ordered goods are paid for after delivery; otherwise, the supplier will know how to defend themselves and initiate and take appropriate measures (e.g., initiate a dunning procedure).

Another style of play is *sequentially* structured, so that a player, like in chess, makes the first move and the fellow player reacts to it, etc. (see also Sect. 6.2.1.2). Such a game setup occurs, for example, in the economy in competitive situations when a company is forced to react to a competitor's marketing activities because the competitor, for instance, tries to penetrate the established market and, for example, opens new branches (see also the example in Fig. 6.1 in this chapter). In classic fashion, the threatened company must then decide between a price war or acceptance of the competing company in its market. A ruinous price war is likely to be negative for both sides and may lead to losses, so that eventually one of the two competing firms must exit the market if it does not want to "go bankrupt." For example, a competition between the two tire manufacturers Goodyear and Michelin took place in the past over entry into the respective local markets of Europe and America, which led to Michelin withdrawing from the American market due to severe losses (see Holler & Klose-Ullmann, 2007, p. 32 f.).

Therefore, caution is advised when analyzing game situations. One must not blindly infer from one game situation (e.g., the Prisoner's Dilemma; see Fig. 6.4) to a completely different constellation, such as the competitive situation of a duopoly here. Holler and Klose-Ullmann (2007, p. 33) rightly pointed out in the aforementioned "Goodyear-Michelin case" that this case did not fit the conditions of the "Prisoner's Dilemma" game, as Michelin was forced to withdraw from the American car market due to high losses, and Goodyear is still active in the European market today and earns "good money" there.

It is always better to reach an understanding that leads to cooperation or agreement or to a market division at reasonable prices, from which both market participants benefit, thus sufficiently participating in the *total profit*. It would be helpful for selecting the game strategy to outline the game options using a decision tree and thus clarify the starting position and proceed "chronologically-logically."

Sequential games also know a special variant called the "Dictator Game" or "Ultimatum Game". In the setup of the Ultimatum Game, the first player is allowed to make a proposal, which the other player must either accept or reject. Only with the fellow player's consent does the payout occur and thus the utilization of benefits; otherwise, neither receives anything, and both players go "empty-handed." In this game variant, that is, in the ultimatum to accept or reject the distribution proposal, it is about the principle: "Take or leave it!"—for both parties. In contrast to the Ultimatum Game, the Dictator Game *does not* depend on the fellow player's consent, but the first and proposing player decides for themselves and autonomously—and their fellow player has no influence on the game process, i.e., for example, on the distribution of the money or assets, and must live with the proposed solution and see where they stand.

In research, for example, the *Ultimatum Game* is played with the instruction:

> "Imagine you have lost your wallet with 100 € and a finder thankfully returns it to you. How much reward would you give them?"

From a strictly rational point of view, an offer of just 1 euro should already be acceptable, because 1 € is better than nothing! For reasons of fairness, however, some (or even many) test subjects would consider a much higher amount justified, ideally even "fifty: fifty," that is, in this case, 50 € as the same amount of money for both sides. Regardless of how the distribution offer turns out, the Nash equilibrium lies in the other player's acceptance of this proposal.

In real life, this ultimatum game could occur in inheritance arrangements, where the testator asks the heirs (e.g., two parties) to agree on a proposal. One of the heirs is then to make a proposal on how the inheritance is to be divided, and the second heir must agree to the outcome; otherwise, both heirs "come away empty-handed" and receive nothing.

However, it should be noted that this game realistically comes into play only from a less close degree of kinship, e.g., degree of kinship III in the relationship between uncle or aunt and nephew or niece, where there is neither a compulsory portion for an heir nor the possibility of contesting the will (such as in Germany).

Regardless of the legal aspects, this game instruction can be an effective method to avoid inheritance disputes after the will is opened. Otherwise, conflicts or resentments may arise, possibly in connection with contestation lawsuits among the (potential) heirs, guaranteed to occur when some of the heirs feel disadvantaged and believe they have been treated or considered unfairly. If, as in a kinship relationship with an uncle or aunt, no contestation lawsuit is possible, so that one or some nephews or nieces receive and inherit everything and the others receive nothing for inexplicable reasons, the previously amicable and peaceful family relationship is likely to have come to an end. At the very least, prior communication about the intended inheritance arrangement would help avoid disputes and counteract and prevent feelings of inadequacy.

6.2.3 Other Game Theory Concepts

With the game theory approaches mentioned so far, the spectrum of game theory concepts is not yet exhausted. On the contrary, there are still many important fields of application in the economy, politics, and "on the social stage" of societal actions where game theory can provide explanations. Whether on a small scale, such as in the private life of a partnership or family, or on a large scale of a collective, it is always about achieving a balance of interests acceptable to both sides, which is to be accomplished through negotiations and mutual agreements (see also Sect. 10.3.2).

Also not to be forgotten is the natural world, that is, biology with its evolutionary events and developments. In evolutionary research, it is not for nothing that it is said: "Survival of the Fittest," when the one with the best or optimal survival strategy prevails! From a game-theoretical perspective, this is nothing other than a Nash equilibrium, from which the "selfish genes" (Dawkins, 1978) and their progeny benefit.

Regardless of the variety of play styles, there are also game approaches that may not necessarily be understood and named as "games per se," such as auctions or bidding.

6.2.3.1 Balance of Interests through Mutual Agreement or Negotiation

Similar to the aforementioned cooperative games, or specifically the ultimatum game, games can lead to achieving a balance of interests through agreements or negotiations. Such games are a comprehensive field of application to achieve a balance of interests or compromise as a result, regardless of the subject matter.

According to the "game theorists," the negotiation result is exactly the Nash equilibrium, which "settles" even with incomplete information about the respective preferences or expectations (see Schelling, 1960/2011, p. 167 ff.). Binmore (2007, p. 145 ff.) provided a nice illustrative example of a newly married couple who had to agree on the distribution of upcoming housework. Previously, the woman, as a single, invested 2 hours every day, i.e., 14 hours a week, in (her) housework. Her husband, previously in his single household, only 1 hour per day, which meant 7 hours a week as an effort. The Nash equilibrium and thus a fair compromise for both sides would be as follows:

"1) Add or sum up the previous time efforts for housework, i.e., 14 + 7 = 21 hours;
2) Divide the time effort of 21 hours by 2, i.e., 21:2 = 10.5 hours;
3) At 10.5 hours, the woman would work 3.5 hours less compared to the previous 14 hours, and her husband only 3.5 hours, as more than 14 hours for housework weekly is not required. Both would have fairly shared the saved time in a joint household."

It should not be surprising that, as with the ultimatum game, the solution or compromise is to be sought and found in the context of a 50:50 distribution, which embodies a balance according to current logic. Deviations from this are to be expected when the previous starting position, i.e., the status quo, is considered and factored into the advantage-disadvantage calculation or the calculation, as the aforementioned example illustrated. From an ideological point of view, this result, valued as a "fair compromise," could also be anything but fair and balanced, as the man halves his domestic work effort, i.e., from 7 to 3.5 hours weekly, while the woman only reduces it by 25% from 14 to 10.5 hours per week.

Different preferences of the individuals involved in negotiation are also effective in another *extended* concept called *"empathetic preferences"* (see Binmore, 2005, pp. 113 ff.). Empathetic preferences take into account social, interpersonal aspects and relationships and could function as a kind of minimum expectation for the negotiation outcome to be achieved, while simultaneously providing emotional understanding for the needs or concerns of the other side. Not least, empathetic preferences have the function of discovering the "critical threshold" of the opponent by "immersing oneself in their situation (or their shoes)" and detecting it depending on the prevailing emotional state. Such a threshold or "cut off" would still be acceptable to the other side and would result in a balanced compromise proposal (see also Binmore, 2009, pp. 70 ff.). Generally speaking, they would be the "last offer" going to the pain threshold (for both sides).

6.2 Games and Their Strategic Calculations

Compromise solutions through the involvement of third parties as mediators or moderators are likely to orient themselves to such a starting position and incorporate it into their calculation or transform it into a possible utility calculation. This could then generally look and function as follows:

"1) *Initial situation of the negotiating parties:* Each negotiation partner has both a *personal* preference or utility scale and an additional *empathetic* utility scale with its own scaling, i.e., with completely different values of utility.
2) *Relationship between personal and empathetic utility scale:* Each scale value of a personal preference currently corresponds to a specific scale value of the possibly parallel existing empathy scale—and vice versa.
3) *Transformation and changes:* Depending on the degree of willingness to compromise or other external influences, these two scales can shift against each other. Thus, a "scaling back" of personal preferences, for example, leads to an increase or enhancement of the empathetic preference and thus to a better or good offer for the other party from the provider's perspective.
4) *Compromise as equilibrium and negotiation solution:* When a compromise is reached, a balance or equilibrium of the negotiating parties' interests is achieved, as Binmore (2005, p. 155) has graphically illustrated."

An empathetic utility scale is probably nothing more than a vehicle or transmission belt from personal utility expectations or preferences into the needs or reality of the other partner, to achieve a compromise acceptable to both sides. Binmore (2009, pp. 70 ff.) mentions that the respective actor is compelled to construct a *new* personal utility scale based on the empathy felt for their counterpart. Empathetic preferences strongly resemble constructs related to prosocial behavior (see Chap. 9).

If the affected parties must come to an agreement among themselves because there is no higher authority or mediator, the principle of "fairness" applies in our culture to reach a balance or equilibrium of interests. It should be noted in the discussion about fairness that this principle or construct is to be understood and perceived purely subjectively and never follows objective or physical criteria.

In practice, for example, complaints may come into the focus of empathetic preferences and need to be addressed from this perspective. A service or invoice that a customer complains about requires the empathetic preference of the service provider or supplier by putting themselves in the customer's position, so to speak, "walking in their shoes," and adjusting their personal preferences or expectations accordingly, accommodating the customer through empathetic preferences. Ideally, the problem would be resolved through a compromise.

With the concept of empathetic preferences, distributions may also be addressed that do not initially intend equal distribution, but rather, for example, due to different competencies, efforts, or power relations, aim for and suggest unequal distributions. A good example is hunting, where the hunt leader claims a larger share of the catch due to their leadership role, which is accepted by their companions, as their skills and experience in leading the hunters present enabled a successful hunt with additional catch in the first place. Thus, in a collective hunt, such as a drive hunt, a completely different "yield" is possible than if each individual hunter goes hunting separately and perhaps returns with only a (small) piece of game. In literature, the comparison "Stag Hunt Game," i.e., the (collective) deer hunt, vs. "Hare," i.e., the hare hunt of an individual hunter, is often used and cited (see Binmore, 2005, p. 67).

"Stag Hunt" can furthermore exemplify the mutual dependency in joint ventures, such as the stag hunt here. According to this formation, for a successful stag hunt, several, or at least two hunters, would be necessary. As soon as one hunter refuses and prefers solo hunting (of a hare), his companion can either join him and go hare hunting himself or end up empty-handed. The Nash equilibria thus lie either in the joint stag hunt (with higher payoff or benefit for both parties) or in the separately conducted hare hunt (see Osborne, 2004, pp. 20 f. and 29 f.). Some individuals might prefer the seemingly safe "smaller prey" (here the hare) in other situations because they adhere to the principle, "a bird in the hand is worth two in the bush," or: "than the pigeon on the roof" (how German people would like to say) which vividly reflects the two Nash equilibria.

6.2.3.2 Auctions

Auctions are of great interest, on the one hand, because of their economic motives or utility calculations, and on the other hand, due to the psychological mechanisms and processes operating and unfolding in the background, particularly the escalation effects caused by competitive bidding leading to ever higher bids, as well as the mutual attempts at influence triggered by this. Focused on the manipulation processes occurring there, the question arises, in particular, who influences whom—or possibly themselves?

Accordingly, a bidder can be strongly manipulated or pressured by their desires. Likewise, he or she can be strongly influenced by other auction participants present and may possibly engage in an excessive "bidding competition," which he or she might later regret if, in the heat of the moment, a too high price for the "object of desire," such as the offered artwork or a special collector's item, becomes due and has to be paid.

It should be noted that in such situations, which are later regretted, it is more likely to assume irrational behavior rather than that the bids followed a rational calculation. For rational bidders, game theorists have developed the following concept:

"1) Each bidder sets an absolute price ceiling as a limit before the auction, which he or she will not exceed. This would then be the individual, personal value of the object to be auctioned.
2) Below this price ceiling, each bidder defines an "ideal price," which represents the desired and best possible deal for the participant (e.g., 30% below the limit as a so-called "bargain").
3) At the beginning, the auctioneer opens with a minimum price, as is customary in the "English auction," which from the seller's perspective represents the

extreme limit "downwards," i.e., the so-called "floor" as the price floor, and is most likely immediately outbid by the bidders, since this price, as already mentioned, is set too low under normal conditions and is more to be understood as a "bait."

4) It is hardly surprising that the ongoing bidding process exceeds each interested party's "ideal price" (see here point 2) sooner or later, and from this bid, the individual speculative gain is diminished until the highest personal price limit is reached, and with disciplined behavior, it would actually be time to exit.

5) However, it is the case that the emerging emotions and desires could take over the "scepter of action," so that the previous ("iron") resolutions no longer apply, and the bidding behavior becomes autonomous with the consequence that it is impossible for the bidder to stop, and he or she successively places further bids, as the desire to ultimately succeed in this auction overshadows and ignores everything else."

As Binmore (2007, p. 114) sardonically noted, it can be a pleasure for observing researchers to watch the mutually infectious emotional processes and influence maneuvers among the subjects in the experiment, as if they were happening in real life.

Irrational pressure, from which irrational overbidding results, occurs due to the unbridled individual urge to win and succeed. Added to this is the perceived and burdensome experience of *scarcity*, when the auction object is unique, like a one-of-a-kind artwork, as well as the *competitive situation* of several auction participants, all wanting the same thing.

From a game-theoretical perspective, individual behavior and experience in pricing are dependent both on one's own motivational forces and on the behavior of the competition or fellow bidders. The bidder who ultimately succeeds and acquires the object must live with his decision; it is for him something like his "steady state," something final, and his personal "Nash equilibrium"!

It is also common for the auctioneer to charge a participation fee for attending all planned auctions of the day, so that for the bidders, at least the attendance fee would be a loss to lament if they do not succeed with any auction object. Such an expense naturally finds its way into the individual "profit-and-loss calculation (P&L calculation)."

Similarly, it would be the case when participating in "American auctions," where the individual bid over the last offered price must be paid in any case, and with a subsequent higher bid, the bidder's money is lost as a stake. In these "all-pay auctions," the focus is more on collecting a large sum of money for charitable purposes than on the appropriate price for acquiring the offered object.

6.2.3.3 Social Contracts as a Game Concept

It may be surprising that normal and natural forms of life are understood and defined as games, as Binmore (2007, p. 85) suggested with the care of elderly family members (or generally speaking, the older generation). Behind this example lies the well-known "generational contract," which concerns the unconditional maintenance and care of the elderly, no longer working people of a society and on which our current social or better alimentation system is based.

As is well known, in ancient times, people lived in extended families over several generations, in family associations or clans. From the harvests or the animals killed during hunting, those who were not involved and no longer active naturally received their share for survival (so to speak, as a "pension").

According to Binmore (2007), this life situation can be represented "playfully" as follows:

"1) Suppose, in this fictional game, each player of an age cohort or generation receives *two* loaves of bread, which they can either consume themselves, i.e., "breakfast," or share with their parents (or a parent). Saving or storing a loaf of bread for old age is not possible, as the bread would spoil and become inedible.
2) An equilibrium in the sense of game theory exists when the young generation (i.e., the daughter or son) shares the received bread with the parents in this phase of life, which according to current theory would be beneficial for both sides and, in principle, without alternative. If this does not happen, the parents would suffer and even starve and would have no other way to repay or avenge this misdeed during their lifetime.
3) However, in game theory, the principle "Tit for Tat" applies, i.e., "As you do to me, so I do to you" (see Sect. 6.2.2.2), so that the daughter or son can later be punished by their own children of the next generation through food deprivation for their omitted and refused assistance and for their unfair behavior.
4) This behavioral principle for neglected care of needy older people acts as a deterrent to the social community or society as a whole, so that nonconformists must expect to be sanctioned or punished later for their unfair behavior."

It is therefore assumed that this system of mutual dependence and cooperation, which is in a state of equilibrium with the conforming behavior of all community members or family members, is stabilized due to mutual benefit across generations and becomes a social or cultural achievement. Manipulative maneuvers then occur through the overarching "system itself" or its instances or principles.

The well-known "pay-as-you-go system," established today in social systems, follows this principle on a supra-individual or societal level by attempting to guarantee the adherence to the "generational contract" in social security or alimentation systems through constant adjustment.

6.2.3.4 Looking into the Abyss: Dealing with Dangerous "Cliffs" and Imbalances ("Brinkmanship")

Politics is not only, but sometimes unfortunately also overshadowed and characterized by military confrontations or conflicts. The security and integrity of the country, its inhabitants, and the prevailing state system are the top priorities or maxims of the head of state or the government entrusted with it. In the event of a tangible dispute that can escalate into an armed conflict, two national governments or state blocs, such as NATO on one side and the former Warsaw Pact on the other, face each other and act in dependence on the assumed or alleged intentions of the opposing side in their own interest. In view of today's high armament with nuclear weapons, the armament primarily serves retaliation, i.e., the "second-strike capability" in the event of a first attack. In this ability to retaliate lies also the deterrence as a threat to potential attackers.

However, heads of state with their command authority are moving on "thin ice," as misunderstandings, misinterpretations, or technical defects, i.e., so-called "false alarms," can never be ruled out in terms of possible military confrontations, so that it cannot always be assumed that there is a malicious and deliberate intention of an opposing party.

This was particularly evident in the past with the emergence of the "1st World War" before the declaration of war on August 1, 1914, where the responsible governments, mainly the monarchies in Russia, Austria-Hungary, and Germany at the time, organized themselves in various alliance systems and, partly out of vanity or special power or particular interests, did not ensure a de-escalation of the conflict to preserve peace as the "highest good." The historian Barbara Tuchman (1962/2013) illustratively traced and documented the "sliding into catastrophe," i.e., into the 1st World War.

Many years later, this situation at that time was the "blueprint" for the American President, John F. Kennedy, on how a game at the brink or a "game with the abyss" (Dixit & Nalebuff, 1995, p. 199) as a gradually escalating conflict should not be handled, which then led to a completely different outcome during the Cuban Missile Crisis in 1962.

For some thoughtful scientists committed to rational action, such as Thomas Schelling (1960/2011), it was a concern to analyze such threatening, escalating political conflicts using the tools of game theory and to understand their dynamics—and possibly to provide important insights to the responsible politicians or commanders. Much in these just-described political-military conflicts reminds one of the so-called phenomenon of "Brinkmanship." The concept known in the English-speaking world as "brink of war" thus involves managing "on the edge of an abyss (or here, war)" with the aim of unsettling the aggression-hungry opponent by manipulating a risk that is to be brought about or is emerging towards disaster, so that he seeks an acceptable way out of the precarious situation for himself, preventing a military confrontation and the possible "great catastrophe" from which he himself would be harmed and possibly destroyed.

Figuratively, "Brinkmanship" can be imagined as a situation of moving adversaries before or at the edge of a cliff (thus staggering in this direction through their maneuvering and actions), which is located at the end of a sloping plane, and in which each new step gains more momentum and the possible consequences become riskier. Both sides thus cling to the abyss and subject themselves to the influence of the situation as they understand it, and at some point, they unintentionally lose all control, and the negative developments to be feared could take on a life of their own. This risk is intended to become increasingly unbearable for the addressee with a hostile attitude, so that he feels more comfortable when he stops his actions and gradually retreats and defuses existing risks.

While before the start of World War I, the acting parties were unable to "jump over their shadows" and take the initiative for a problem or conflict resolution, and on the other hand, to properly understand and perceive the threat of this escalating situation, the Americans made it unmistakably clear to the Soviets during the Cuban Missile Crisis that if they continued their activities, i.e., broke through and violated the naval blockade off Cuba, they would have to reckon with all conceivable consequences and risks. The incalculable risks for the Soviets lay not only in the intentions and decisions of the American president but also in the processes occurring under his command within the military subordinate to him—and that at all levels. Of course, there was the additional uncertainty for the aggressor of not being able to calculate how far the American president would be willing to go in the extreme case.

Manipulations in such a dangerous situation for both sides aim to dampen the expectations of successful action for the opponent and to push and entangle him in incalculable risks that prompt him to reassess the situation and thus "reverse" his actions. Thus, it would ultimately be more advantageous for the aggressor to de-escalate and undertake an orderly retreat, even if this might be difficult for him for reasons of image.

Psychologically, threats thus have the purpose of deterring the opponent and, paradoxically as it sounds, prompting him to act in such a way out of fear of escalation—and his own disadvantages or even destruction—that the threat does not lead to action. The threatening party must also commit itself to this and let it shine through unmistakably to be credible.

Deterrence, on the other hand, as a complement to the threat, means, on the one hand, the ability to retaliate at any time even after an unexpected first strike, i.e., the so-called "second-strike capability," which also destroys the aggressor (e.g., as a state or country) after the first strike. On the other hand, it refers to the incalculable risk for an opponent, either generally or from "false alarms," which could also unintentionally lead to catastrophe if he or she pushes the escapades to the limit.

6.3 Summary

Obviously, the "universe" of strategy games seems inexhaustible, so the initially presented "classic" strategy games, such as the economic situation of two oligopolists (duopolists) in a defined common market or the legendary games like the Prisoner's Dilemma or the so-called Chicken Game, represent only a small excerpt from the diversity of games.

Games that also function as distinct concepts with their own game orientation or purpose, such as "Battle of the Sexes," also known as "Bach or Stravinsky," or colloquially expressed as "Cinema or Football," were not presented and discussed. In this game, it is crucial for both players to decide on an option together to stay together and not go separate ways in their leisure activities (for example, if the

6.3 Summary

woman goes to the cinema and the man to the football game). In the game "Public Goods," as another well-known game concept, it is about the exploitation of natural resources, such as a pasture or meadow. For grazing a herd, only a certain number of grazing animals is allowed on this (public) meadow if the meadow is to regenerate after grazing, which every shepherd is aware of, and he must not enrich himself at the expense of others or the community.

As already touched upon in the strategy approaches and game forms, the games can be distinguished and classified according to various categories, such as "zero-sum games" (also called non-cooperative games) vs. "non-zero-sum games" or cooperative games. Furthermore, a distinction can be made between "pure strategies," i.e., games with an alternative decision like "yes" or "no," or "mixed strategies," which work with probability assumptions. Finally, games have a specific character depending on their environment or area of application, whether they deal with economic questions or problems or whether they address certain conflicts in the field of justice or criminology or in politics (including military and society).

Regardless of these differentiations and specific game styles, there are also game approaches that may not necessarily be understood and called a "game in itself," such as auctions or bidding. In all these game concepts, it ultimately comes down to achieving a balance of interests through negotiations or agreements or to prevail or achieve the best possible outcome depending on the possible reactions of the opposing party, which pursues the same goal (i.e., to reach a so-called Nash equilibrium). In these obvious or hidden interdependencies between the actors involved in the game lies the potential for manipulation to influence each other, which comes into play especially with threats and deterrence regarding retaliatory measures.

"System Diagnostics" of Dependency Relationships and Mutual Influence Attempts

In the individual diagnostics of specific questions or problems for individual respondents, this project could be implemented in various ways (see Chap. 5). Either solely through a conversation or, in individual cases, by using personality tests or other survey instruments such as checklists or similar. If these test procedures included a lie scale, the truthfulness of the responses given or the manipulation-based "social desirability" could at least be controlled and roughly assessed in terms of interpreting the test results in personality traits.

For the "system diagnostics" of playful processes or interactions, with the already highlighted interdependencies in the strategic behavior of the players, there is naturally no procedure comparable to personality tests. For diagnostics or analysis of the (game) events, either only the observation and recording of behavior or the "moves" (e.g., also via film recording or video recording) is available as the method of choice, or it is possible to simulate and test the possible course of the game a priori within the framework of previous simulations or experiments (e.g., as a computer simulation like in chess). Prospectively, a "system diagnostics" in the sense understood here represents a kind of "meta-analysis," which attempts, from a superior perspective, i.e., bird's-eye or helicopter view, to anticipate the current events or the upcoming moves or reactions of the participants based on the assumed or presumed interests or preferences and to deterministically narrow down and capture the possible and most likely game outcome or, as best as possible, to predict it.

As a result of these strategic considerations, the possible utility expectations (i.e., the "payoffs" in the fields of the payoff matrix) for the decision or strategy constellations in question, taking into account the possible reactions of the fellow player, should be quantified or assessed as a rough "limit value consideration." At the very least, as already mentioned in the previous chapter (see Sect. 6.2.1.2), the preferences of the actors should be highlighted in an ordinal scale or in a system ordered by ranks. Not to be underestimated in any interaction or game constellation are the psychological determinants and aspects, which particularly stand out and come into play with regard to possible manipulation attempts.

As already presented (see Sect. 6.2.2), there is a multitude of game variants, each revealing their own "laws" as game possibilities. As far as it is sensible and necessary, reference should be made to this in the following explanation of the analysis or diagnostics of game approaches as needed. Otherwise, in this Chap. 7, it is more about system analysis, which initially orients itself to the "anatomy" of games per se, and on the other hand, about certain types of games that are suitable for analysis from a psychodiagnostic perspective due to the typically human thought and behavior patterns. Finally, special specific methods provide approaches for a completely different kind of system analysis, such as the "signal detection theory" or portfolio techniques, which differ from diagnostics of games or moves.

7.1 System Analysis and System Diagnostics of the Anatomy of Games

In principle, in a game, two opposing players or parties have to decide on one decision alternative each. If player (A) chooses decision (X) instead of (Y), for example, he plays strategy (XA), and not (YA), regardless of how his fellow player decides or reacts (see Fig. 7.1). The same situation applies to the fellow player (B) as the initial situation, who plays his strategy "MB" or "NB".

Without an idea of what consequences or results of the possible alternative decisions or strategies are to be expected in the end, a game fundamentally makes no sense. Thus, it is necessary to calculate or estimate the expected utility of a chosen strategy to arrive at a personal preference for further moves. Not infrequently, the expected utility values (= U) result in a decision dilemma, namely when their outcome depends on the reaction or counter-reaction of the fellow player (see Fig. 7.2).

Thus, for player (A), decision (Y) would be the best decision, but only if the fellow player (B) votes for decision (M). This would be rather unexpected with an

Player: A (rows) / B (columns)	Decision "M"	Decision "N"
Decision "X"	Strategy "MB" Strategy "XA"	Strategy "NB" Strategy "XA"
Decision "Y"	Strategy " MB" Strategy "YA"	Strategy "NB" Strategy "YA"

Fig. 7.1 From Decision to Strategy

7.1 System Analysis and System Diagnostics ...

Player: A (rows) / B (columns)	Decision "M"	Decision "N"
Decision "X"	U = 3 U = 3	U = 2 U = 2
Decision "Y"	U = 1 U = 4	U = 4 U = 1

Fig. 7.2 Decision and Payoff Matrix with Different Utility Values

expected payoff of U = 1 for player (B). If player (B) instead chooses variant (N), the result for player (A) would even reverse, and player (B) would have the benefit that player (A) had previously desired.

Thus, with the same level of information, it is expected that player (A) will prefer decision option (X) and player (B) will opt for alternative (M), as it represents the best outcome (or an equilibrium) for both actors due to the dependency relationship. It should also be noted that this constellation is ambivalent for both players and would be their best possible decision, as neither of the two actors possesses a "dominant strategy" that he or she would play in any case, regardless of how the opposing side behaves.

The starting point of all considerations should therefore be the question of whether there is a "dominant strategy" for one of the players. If it exists, it also provides him with a Nash equilibrium. Consequently, and logically, every player will play a dominant strategy, as it is without alternative for him. The other player only has the option to choose his "best response" without influencing the behavior of the other (dominant) player. If there is no dominant strategy, as in this example in Fig. 7.2, the search for an equilibrium of the game necessarily begins (see Dixit & Nalebuff, 1995, pp. 60 ff., 67 and 76).

The possible moves to be taken are not always equally probable, i.e., discrete events that either occur or do not occur if not considered. Therefore, probability assumptions (see Fig. 7.3) about the occurrence of this event are sometimes necessary from the "strategists." For example, if player (A) expects a probability (p) of 70% (or 0.70) for a result in a decision (X), according to applicable logic, the counter-probability $(1 - p)$ for the non-occurrence of this result or event must be $(1 - 0.70 = 0.30)$ or 30%. This would then be the probability statement for the occurrence of the result in a decision (Y). In the same way, player (B) calculates the expected probabilities (q) depending on his chosen decision (M) or (N).

It is easy to see in Fig. 7.3 that the utility expectation from Fig. 7.2 has merely been supplemented by the probability assumptions.

Based on these a priori created decision and payoff matrices, the game outcome can be assessed and tentatively quantified depending on the possible game constellations, in order to arrive at a "best possible" or optimal strategy, thereby

Player: A (rows) / B (columns)	Decision "M"	Decision "N"
Decision "X"	(U = 3) x q (U = 3) x p	(U = 2) x (1-q) (U = 2) x p
Decision "Y"	(U = 1) x q (U = 4) x (1-p)	(U = 4) x (1-q) (U = 1) x (1-p)

Fig. 7.3 Decision and payoff matrix with different utility values and probability assumptions

concluding the system analysis or system diagnostics in the sequence of these procedural steps.

Nash equilibria in "mixed strategies" also mean that with pairs of probabilities, such as (p) or (1 − p), none of the participants can achieve a higher utility than with these expected probabilities (see Holler & Klose-Ullmann, 2007, p. 155), which is expressed by weighting the utility values with their probabilities.

Unlike with complete or perfect information about the initial situation of the game (as shown in Fig. 7.2), with *imperfect information*, which is based on uncertain situation assessments, auxiliary assumptions or conjectures must be made or consulted (as done in Fig. 7.3). Uncertainties can best be expressed through probability statements or expectations and used for calculated decision-making or for identifying an equilibrium. Probabilities are generally based on *subjective* probability estimates, so to speak, "to the best of one's knowledge and belief," if no other or more accurate information is available.

It should generally be noted that for determining utility expectations or payoffs, Bernoulli's approach is the method of choice (as already undertaken and shown in Fig. 7.3). In this procedure, both the expected utility values of the desired or preferred event can be weighted with the assumed probability of occurrence (p), and the alternatively possible outcomes can be added to an expected value using the same procedure with their "counter-probability" (1 − p).

Using the game "Battle of the Sexes," where the aim is to agree on a joint leisure activity, such as cinema or football, the situation of a player who is unclear about the preferences of his fellow player (B) can be exemplarily demonstrated (this numerical example, from which only the numbers were taken for comparison reasons, can be found in Osborne, 2004, pp. 273 ff.).

In contrast to the previous application example (see Fig. 7.3), a player faces fundamentally alternative initial situations that he must incorporate into his strategic planning considerations.

To keep the calculation simple, player (A) assumes a probability (p) of 0.5 or 50% each that player (B) will choose alternative 1 (e.g., to meet = yes) or alternative 2 (e.g., not to meet = no). The calculation of the expected utility values of player (A) then looks as shown in Fig. 7.6.

7.1 System Analysis and System Diagnostics ...

As a result, for player (A), the utility values weighted by their probability of entry of 0.5 arise depending on the decision combination of the fellow player (B). If player (B) knows which preference structure player (A) prefers or has, player (B) has complete or perfect information with the payoff values from the payoff matrices of Figs. 7.4 and 7.5. By comparing the utility values of players (A) and (B) from Figs. 7.4 and 7.5, the possible equilibria can be determined (see Fig. 7.6).

If player (A) plays the strategy "X", an equilibrium with the combination of M1 and N2 from player (B) with U = 1 would be expected; however, if he plays

Player: A (rows) / B (columns)	Decision "M1"	Decision "N1"
Decision "X1"	1 2	0 0
Decision "Y1"	0 0	2 1

Fig. 7.4 Payoff matrix for player (A) in the case that the fellow player (B) wants to coordinate (Alternative 1)

Player: A (rows) / B (columns)	Decision "M2"	Decision "N2"
Decision "X2"	0 2	2 0
Decision "Y2"	1 0	0 1

Fig. 7.5 Payoff matrix for player (A) in the case that the fellow player (B) does not want to coordinate (Alternative 2)

	Combinations from player B	M1 and M2	M1 and N2	N1 and M2	N1 and N2
Calculations of player A	for X1 and X2	½ x 2 + ½ x 2 = 2	½ x 2 + ½ x 0 = 1	½ x 0 + ½ x 2 = 1	½ x 0 + ½ x 0 = 0
	for Y1 and Y2	½ x 0 + ½ x 0 = 0	½ x 0 + ½ x 1 = 1/2	½ x 1 + ½ x 0 = 1/2	½ x 1 + ½ x 1 = 1

Fig. 7.6 Calculation of the weighted utility values of player (A)

the strategy "Y", the combination for player (A) of N1 and N2 from player (B) would present itself as an equilibrium (see Osborne, 2004, p. 278).

According to Binmore (2005), the following initial conditions must also be distinguished when calculating the utility (U):

> "1) Orientation towards mutual maximum total utility (according to the utility principle)
> According to Fig. 7.2, the total utility is maximal in the decision constellation "X" (for player A) and "M" (for player B), as is easily recognizable, with $3 + 3 = 6$ when adding the utility values and with multiplication $3 \times 3 = 9$, which is neither reached nor surpassed by any other decision combination in the payoff matrix. Multiplying the utility scores is sensible and necessary if the status quo is to be included in the calculation. If the status quo as a starting value for both players was, for example, "1", the following calculation would apply:
> $(3 − 1) \times (3 − 1) = 4$ as total utility for both players (see Binmore, 2005, p. 26).
> It is easy to see that this total utility, considering the status quo, is not reached by any other decision combination in this example.
> 2) Orientation with different weightings or preferences of the players ("social indices" according to Binmore, 2005, pp. 29 f.)
> Assuming player (A) has a preference (or a "social index") of 2 and thus a claim to utility twice as high as his fellow player (B), the following result would arise in this calculation:
> 3/2 (for A) + 3/1 (for B) = 1.5 + 3 = 4.5 (as total utility and weighting)
> In this calculation, the utility for player (A) would be lower than for player (B), yet it is overall the best possible result.
> 3) Orientation towards equal shares (according to the equality principle) and considering the status quo
> Considering equal (egalitarian) shares results in a completely different calculation, namely (where the status quo for both games is also "1"):
> $(3 − 1) = (3 − 1)$ or $2 = 2$
> 4) Considering personal preferences (or weightings), the calculation would look as follows (see also point 2 of these example calculations) and would fundamentally no longer meet the equality requirement:
> $(3 − 1)/2 = (3 − 1)/1$ or $1 = 2$ or $1:2$."

According to Binmore (2005, p. 33), the proponents of utilitarianism ignore the status quo, while the egalitarians always take it into account. When oriented towards the utility or utilitarian principle, it seems to be solely about the possible gain or added value as an overall or common result, whereas the proponents of the equality or egalitarian principle place great value on fairness and justice. Considering the status quo, the extent of change compared to the status quo is therefore crucial.

At first glance, the aforementioned calculations seem simple and trivial, as the so-called "four basic arithmetic operations" are completely sufficient in terms of mathematical knowledge, regardless of whether the status quo or any weighting factors are included in the calculation.

Binmore (2005) expanded the existing framework of game theory with his discussions on the utility principle and equality principle to include moral-philosophical and social conditions for interactive actions between different people and attempted to offer procedural approaches for solving contentious problems (see also Chap. 9). Thus, Binmore created additional perspectives or viewpoints for a system analysis.

Crucial for the "system diagnostics" is also the initial situation, that is, whether the decisions are to be made simultaneously and without possible coordination or mutual observations of the parties, or whether the decisions are made sequentially, so that one player has taken note of the previous decision of their fellow player and can react accordingly (see also the previous Chap. 6). Which decision constellation is present often depends on the substantive problems of the given situation itself.

7.2 Selected Games and Their Analysis

With the already listed decision and payoff matrices, some deep insights into the game setup of strategy games could be conveyed without considering the game variant. However, another influencing factor on the gameplay of such games is the substantive situational problems, which have already been pointed out elsewhere (see Sect. 6.2). Accordingly, it makes a considerable difference whether it is an economic problem in the market processing of competing companies or whether we are dealing with the deterrence of a conceivable military conflict between two states or defense alliances. Not only the possible "payoffs" as decision or action consequences may not be comparable, but also the situational conditions may differ massively from each other and evoke completely different initial situations and thus completely different action maxims as consequences.

Regardless of situational differences and problems, it is inevitable in this context of a system analysis that the following games or episodes from "everyday life" regarding the preferences in the payoff matrices could partially overlap with the prototypes of games from the previous Chap. 6in their structure and preparation.

7.2.1 Damage Regulation

A nice and frequently occurring example from practice is damage regulation or the claims of the injured party (or the victim) in the event of damage caused by another person (or the perpetrator) (e.g., during or after a traffic accident), which are often settled and regulated by a magistrate either through a settlement or decided by judgment. The starting point is the already mentioned balance of interests, which ends as a problem solution or compromise, which can also be an arbitration or judgment by a higher instance, and with a "balanced" result or an equilibrium state (see Sect. 6.2.3.1). Of course, the achieved compromise does not automatically ensure or imply that all parties involved are completely satisfied with the negotiation result, as the subsequent example of satisfying a claim for damages illustrates.

After a damage has occurred, such as after a traffic accident, the injured party as the "victim" and the injurer as the perpetrator always face each other. For damage regulation, the question of guilt is also crucial, that is, whether the perpetrator has caused the damage "100%" or whether the injured party is partly to blame and is held accountable. For example, the question of guilt can radically change if the injured traffic participant is proven to have consumed alcohol through a blood test or if he or she does not have or did not have a driver's license.

Apart from clarifying the question of guilt, in the normal case and for the purpose of the analysis or system diagnostics at hand, one can assume a clear situation, e.g., when a driver damages a parked vehicle out of carelessness and the other vehicle owner was not personally present and involved in the accident. At most, the amount of damage would be disputed after consulting an expert or after repairs carried out by a specialist workshop, which would ultimately need to be clarified and decided by a court judgment. If the damage settlement is to be decided either out of court or in the first hearing ("the first instance"), the parties involved face the following initial situation:

> "1) The injured party claims damages of, for example, €10,000. Of this, an undisputed (material) part is due to repair costs, and an immaterial portion is, for example, compensation for pain and suffering or other (alleged) compensations, which are then negotiated or even disputed.
> 2) The injuring party may be willing to satisfy the material claims plus possibly an additional compensation payment to settle the remaining claims, which as a counteroffer is usually below the desired compensation amount (e.g., 60% or €6,000 as in this example).
> 3) Either a solution is reached through bilateral negotiations (with or without legal counsel) or in the course of a lawsuit.
> 4) The preference structure of the disputing parties could be represented as shown in Fig. 7.7:"

From a game-theoretical perspective, the following problem situation may arise depending on the question of guilt, which is decisive for the calculation of the actors (game-deciding) (the utility values U = ... chosen here in Fig. 7.7 are freely chosen):

> "(1) If the injured party bears partial fault or even complete self-fault, the injuring party can assume that they are either not obliged to pay any compensation or at most only a relatively minor amount, regardless of how high the demands of the other side are. For the alleged damage causer, this is a positive result, which is either even more positive than expected or roughly corresponds to their expected compensation payments. The utility can be estimated for them as $U = 2$. For the injured party, the settlement is less positive, as their original claims are not fulfilled, hence $U = 1$.
> (2) If the claimant's demands exactly meet the counterparty's compensation offer, a Nash equilibrium exists, as the expectations of both sides are met and cannot be surpassed by any move. In the aforementioned matrix, the injured party would accept the counteroffer with a payoff of $U = 3$, and they would also psychologically support the offer (therefore $U = 3$ as the greater utility for them compared to $U = 1$, where they could not enforce their original demand). Their opponent gains the greatest personal utility with $U = 4$, because this result is exactly in line with their expectations.
> (3) For the injured party, of course, the settlement of the damage in the desired amount would be a "top result," which would exactly meet their expectations and would be either reluctantly accepted by the opposing party or decided by a court ruling. The psychological utility lies at $U = 4$ for the claimant and at $U = -1$ for the other side, as they must accept this damage claim "with a heavy heart" and come to terms with it, as, for example, the court decided so.

7.2 Selected Games and Their Analysis

Injured party: A (rows) / person causing damage: B (columns)	Settlement of the maximum damage claim (= M)	Settlement of the offered claim (= N)
Demand for maximum Damage claim of € 10,000 (=X)	U = -1 U = 4	U = 2 U = 1
Acceptance of the counteroffer from 6,000 € (=Y)	U = 3 U = -1	U = 4 U = 3

Fig. 7.7 Payout matrix for the case of damage settlement

(4) The psychological state for the damage causer appears ambivalent (therefore $U = 3$), if they are willing to fully settle the damage, but the injured person either makes lower claims or higher claims are rejected by a judicial instance and they are forced to do so. Regardless of whether the damage causer later rejoices over the lower compensation to be paid or not, they would have felt compelled and would have been willing to go beyond the now stated damage claims of the opposing side, thus overcompensating them. A waiver of valid claims is always a priori painful for a claimant, so for the injured party, the situation is psychologically perceived and assessed as $U = -1$."

Incidentally, it may be noted that the opponent B, as the damage causer, can exercise a dominant strategy that absolutely shapes—or even manipulates—the course of the game! In the relevant literature, this case of compensation is also formally and logically represented, where it is particularly noted that an equilibrium is reached in the confrontation of the two demands or counter-demands, which would then be the "best solution" for both sides.

A limitation of the claims for damages by the injured party automatically, that is, by system, exists when or because the claim under normal circumstances and due to the applicable logic can never be exceeded (only in absolutely exceptional situations would later claims, for example, due to later occurring health damages as long-term consequences, be conceivable and possibly permissible).

If the question of guilt is not clearly resolved and results in an allocation of "partial guilt," the following approach would still be relevant and should be carried out as a "side calculation": Purely formally, the expected claim (E) of the parties is to be applied to the determined or assigned share (p) for one party and $(1 - p)$ for the other party, possibly depending on the question of guilt, based on the determined or established damage sum (Z), i.e., to be deducted from it, so that a residual value as compensation between zero (0) and $E - (p \times Z)$ or $E - (1 - p) \times Z$ can result on the opposing side (cf. Osborne, 2004, pp. 91 ff.).

7.2.2 Failure to Render Assistance

Some or even many people are not necessarily malicious or have a "bad character" when they do not care for and strive to help the victims in emergencies. Most of the time, they are carefree and thus comfortable because they more or less rely on the reactions of other people without a "bad conscience."

Many have certainly often heard or even experienced and observed themselves that the larger the number of the randomly present audience, the less is to be expected and thus to be reckoned with that anyone will become active and, for example, make an emergency call in an accident. This phenomenon, known in social psychology as "collective non-responsibility," arises because everyone likes to rely on others to avoid having to become active themselves! Of course, every activity is not only associated with energy but also with "psychological effort" or stress to initiate and set in motion an action and possibly have to justify it afterward.

Game-theoretically, the probability of inactivity with an *increasing* number of people can be represented and proven as a "symmetric mixed equilibrium" (see Fig. 7.8). According to the explanations, for example, by Osborne (2004, pp. 133 f.), the following applies:

> "1) the value for an emergency call is "v" (for value)
> 2) the "psychological effort" is "c" (for cost)
> 3) the payoff for an emergency call is then "v – c" (and the payoff for no emergency call "v – c" = 0)
> 4) the probability (p) for an emergency call is "v × p," and the probability for no emergency call "v × (1 – p)"
> 5) from this, based on the "payoffs" (v – c) and through algebraic transformations, the ratio c/v = –1 + p or p = 1 – c/v results
> 6) and considering the number of people (n), the probability results:
> p = 1 – (c/v) $^{1/n-1}$, that an emergency call is made by any present person
> 7) when the number of people (n) increases, it can be proven that the probability that at least one emergency call occurs continuously decreases; for example, with 2 people (and c/v = 1/4) it applies: p = 1 – (1/4) $^{1/2-1}$ = 1 – 0.25 = 0.75 and for example, with 3 people it applies: p = 1 – (1/4) $^{1/3-1}$ = (1 – 1/2) = 1 – 0.50 = 0.50"

Person: A (lines)/other Person: B (columns)	Emergency call (= M)	No emergency call (= N)
Emergency call (=X)	(v – c) x q (v – c) x p	(v – c) x (1 – q) = 0 (v – c) x p
No emergency call (=Y)	(v – c) x q (v – c) x (1 – p) = 0	(v – c) x (1 – q) = 0 (v – c) x (1 – p) = 0

Fig. 7.8 Payout matrix for the case "Failure to Render Assistance"

Thus, the probability of an emergency call in the example presented here decreases from 75% to 50% with an additional person, now three people instead of two, and the indifference of the present people finds, if you will, its "equilibrium" or "steady state" here. From the perspective of system diagnostics, this is an excellent application example to investigate and analyze the mechanisms of social systems using game theory. Individual characteristics or dispositions are left out or are not the subject of this psychological diagnostics or system diagnostics.

Diffusion of responsibility in connection with the bystander effect was or is one of the most intensive research efforts in social psychology with the best-confirmed experimental findings. Although these are different research hypotheses, the investigations with their results point in the same direction.

Beginning with the tragic murder of the barmaid Kitty Genovese in New York in 1964, where according to press reports, allegedly 38 witnesses perceived the horrific act, either witnessing it or hearing the victim's screams—and no emergency call was made to the police! Initially, there was great astonishment, if not even shock, and complete incomprehension in the public about the failure to provide assistance.

Thus, psychologists Latané and Darley (1968; cited in Levine & Manning, 2014, p. 369 ff.) took the perceived "public echo" as an occasion to investigate the research of this phenomenon "failure to provide assistance" with the hypothesis that more bystanders at an accident or crime scene simultaneously means less willingness to help. Their experiments with simulated epileptic seizures with a) only one person present, b) two people present, and c) more than two people present (in the experiment = 5 people present) demonstrated a declining rate of accident reports with an increasing number of bystanders.

Of all the participants who were alone in the experiment, 15% were not willing to react at all and remained passive. As soon as other test subjects joined, the rate of calls for help dropped from initially (100 − 15 =) 85% with one person present to 62% (with two participants present) and to 31% with several people present (as in this case, e.g., 5 people).

Tendentially, the mathematical approach from game theory seems to correspond to the experimental findings, so that these insights mutually confirmed each other.

7.2.3 Free Riders

In today's work environment, many employees who work together with other colleagues cannot avoid occasionally showing special effort, that is, "putting in extra effort," and working more. Whether through additional overtime or through work quality or productivity, they are particularly challenged, for example, during personnel or scheduling bottlenecks, to lead the joint project to success. This intention does not always find a positive response from all involved, so the necessary extra work is not performed by everyone in the same way. For Osborne

Employees: A (lines)/B (columns)	Overtime	No overtime
Overtime	U = 2 U = 2	U = 3 U = -1
No overtime	U = -1 U = 3	U = 1 U = 1

Fig. 7.9 Extra work or "Free Riding"

(2004, pp. 15 f.), this is a game comparable to the "Prisoner's Dilemma" game and with the same "payoff structure" (see Fig. 7.9).

The situation is perfectly fine when all project employees "pull together" and show the same additional work effort and ambition to ensure the successful completion of the joint project. Consequently, an equilibrium with a utility of $U = 2$ for all involved persons is established. Free riders (or also called slackers or in English "goof offs") are by definition all those who refuse or evade the extra work and let other colleagues work for them. Their utility is then maximized at $U = 3$, while the willing employees not only performed the extra work and brought the project to completion but also had to endure the unpleasant feeling of being exploited or looking like a fool. Therefore, no utility can have arisen for them; rather, the opposite is to be assumed (hence $U = -1$). If all persons involved in the project, so to speak, "let their feet dangle" and let the project slide, the work will not be crowned with success ($U = 1$). All project participants can claim for themselves that they did not overexert themselves too much and beyond measure.

But not only in the working world is there a risk of lack of collegiality or other unpleasant or even fraudulent attacks, also in larger associations or organizations, mean manipulations can occur as "cheating." For example, Dixit and Nalebuff (1995, pp. 332 f.) presented a conceivable deception maneuver within the OPEC organization regarding the agreement on the maximum oil production of these oil-producing countries (the figures were taken from this example, but the presentation in Fig. 7.10 was adjusted and changed).

According to the agreement, Country A is allowed to produce four (4) units of oil and Country B only one (1) unit. Both Country A and Country B might be tempted to secretly produce more, either two units (Country B) or five units (Country A). However, an expansion of production now comes at the expense of the profit margin or revenue. The larger producing Country A thus fares better if it does not react to the "cheating" of producing Country B and keeps its share constant at four units. The utility for Country A would be significantly greater at $U = 48$ than if it reciprocates Country B's deception maneuver and "pays back in kind" ($U = 40$ for Country A and $U = 16$ for Country B).

7.3 Other Possibilities of System Diagnostics

Oil producing countries: A (rows) / B (columns)	Production volume Country B= 1	Production volume Country B = 2	Profit depending on production volume
Production volume Country A = 4	U = 16 U = 64	U = 24 U = 48	16 for quantity 5
Production volume Country A = 5	U = 12 U = 60	U = 16 U = 40	12 for quantity 6
Alternative production volumes:	a) 4 + 1 = 5 c) 5 + 1 = 6	b) 4 + 2 = 6 d) 5 + 2 = 7	8 for quantity 7

Fig. 7.10 Revenue of oil-producing countries depending on production quantity and profit

With the then achieved revenue or profit, a still acceptable result is obtained for both oil producers or countries in this constellation, although this result is anything but optimal for the country (A), as would have been the case if the agreement had been adhered to (with $U = 64$).

7.3 Other Possibilities of System Diagnostics

Apart from the game-theoretical approaches for the analysis or diagnostics of systems and their courses, there are other comparable methodological concepts that are applied for important (rational) decisions. This includes the "Signal Detection Theory" originating from communication technology, which has proven particularly useful in detecting "correct" or "incorrect" signals (and their confusions or errors). Furthermore, in certain situations, samples must be used instead of full surveys for the purpose of verification or control, as such a procedure is simply more economical or pragmatic, and thus an incalculable risk of discovery remains for those affected. Finally, portfolio analysis is an excellent methodology for self-control and strategy planning, so it must not be missing in this context.

7.3.1 Sensitivity Analysis Using "Signal Detection Theory"

For the experimental verification of various psychological performances, such as the performance of sensory organs like the eye, the ear, etc., or attention and concentration abilities, to name just a few among many other areas of investigation, certain measurement procedures with a suitable analysis and evaluation methodology are required. A common procedure, originally developed in engineering sciences and then used in communication technology and the military, is the "Signal Detection Theory" (see e.g., Velden, 1982).

Their application is usually associated with the goal of differentiating between *correct* signals (= hits) and *false* signals, which are perceived and evaluated as correct and accurate or not recognized as false (= false alarms or also called "blind alarm"), in order to determine and assess the performance or capability of the system (e.g., a sensory system like hearing ability). In the studies, subjects still have the opportunity or choice to recognize false signals as such (= correct rejections) or they make the other error of assessing correct signals as false or erroneous (= unrecognized or overlooked correct signals). A prerequisite for sensory performance is that, for example, a tone must have a certain frequency or volume to be perceived or heard at all; otherwise, the subject would signal "no tone" or possibly noise as an accompanying interference noise. In psychophysics, we speak of "just noticeable thresholds or differences" when recognizing barely perceived thresholds, if according to the definition, at least 50% of the stimuli with a certain physical unit or strength (e.g., frequencies in Hz or sound levels in dB) were correctly recognized and perceived as such (cf. Hayos, 1972).

This investigative procedure is also applied in psychological test diagnostics, such as in the "Attention and Concentration Test d2" (originally Brickenkamp, 1962). In this test, a test candidate must distinguish and select between similar symbols as stimulus presentations under time pressure, whether the stimuli are correctly presented or distorted. Depending on how the investigation is designed and conducted, the participant has difficulties or problems recognizing and identifying the desired and correct symbols as such. In other words, with a workload to be managed within a given time span, not only hits but also errors are to be expected, depending on the performance provided and the existing abilities.

The frequency of errors, in particular, is an indication of the risk attitude or risk propensity with which the test candidate, so to speak, "gets to work." Special interest is given to the question of whether he or she processes many tasks superficially with an above-average number of errors or whether accuracy is important to him or her with a relatively low amount of processing. Both risk or work styles have practical relevance and are particularly problem-dependent concerning the consequences of errors that have occurred. For example, the military or air traffic control, due to the expected negative consequences of incorrect object identifications (i.e., disasters or catastrophes), strives to capture all signals or objects accurately on their radar screens and to allow no errors in perception and assessment. In contrast, when checking concentration performance using the "d2" performance test, it would be tolerable for subjects to also make errors, as this is naturally implied in test diagnostics and has no serious consequences.

In medical diagnostics (e.g., in the early detection of tumors using X-rays, such as mammography), it is also unavoidable that malignant findings are not recognized because either the measurements or determinations were faulty or the tumors, due to their small size (in the early stage), were not yet visible and thus not yet diagnosable. Medical diagnostics, in particular, is measured by its *sensitivity* to recognize clinically significant symptoms or abnormalities on the one hand, and uncritical (normal) phenomena on the other, which in technical language is called *specificity*.

7.3 Other Possibilities of System Diagnostics

Stimulus (row)/Person (column)	Reaction = No	Reaction = Yes
Signal	Unrecognized (ß – error) false negative	Hit (1 – ß)
No signal (or "dud")	Correct rejection (1 – α)	False alarms (α) false positive

Fig. 7.11 Test design for investigations with the "Signal Detection Theory"

7.3.1.1 Basic or Measurement Model

The test and test design shown in Fig. 7.11 (see Fig. 7.11) is fundamentally assumed when using signal detection theory as an instrument.

Similar to dealing with the test of hypotheses for falsification, i.e., focusing on the invalidity or rejection of the null hypothesis (H_0), the assessment of signals or alternative (irregular or false) events is also structured. In falsification, the hypothesis tester takes a "negative" basic attitude, aiming to recognize false signals and correctly reject them (= no hits or correct rejections) or, as in hypothesis testing, to reject the null hypothesis in the sense of falsification.

In hypothesis testing, the principal goal is known to be the rejection of the null hypothesis, which then leads to the acceptance or provisional validity of the alternative hypothesis (H_1). The error probability (α) is associated with the idea or assumption of mistakenly rejecting the null hypothesis, even though it is correct and applicable. The probability ($1 - \alpha$) is therefore also the confidence range or confidence interval, with this probability of having made the correct decision.

The same applies to the identification of signals or other critical findings. However, the correct reaction to signal detection would be immediately *yes* (= hit), and the error of mistaking a "dud" for a correct signal is the probability (α) of triggering a "false alarm"—and comparable to hypothesis testing, the probability of rejecting the null hypothesis when it is actually true. Not without reason is the α-error for "false positive" decisions called the probability of error!

In addition, the "correct rejections" are the "no responses" to the "false signals," and the errors occurring here, of overlooking or failing to recognize a signal and also responding with "no," are the "false negative" decisions, also known as Beta errors (β). -In hypothesis testing, the null hypothesis would be mistakenly accepted, even though it is false and incorrect, or the alternative hypothesis (H_1) would be rejected.

When conducting hypothesis tests or detecting and assigning signals, it is also important to note that the two probability functions (of the null hypothesis and the alternative hypothesis) are in a certain relationship to each other and contain a decision criterion (X_c = Cut off) on the "psychological dimension" (e.g., attention to correct or false signals or concentration performance), which is responsible for the subject's decision to indicate either signal or no signal and accurately reflects the sensation or perception of the tested individual. Figuratively speaking, two normal distributions are present as "Gaussian bell curves" (ordinate), which intersect at the criterion (X_c) on the psychological dimension (abscissa). Technically interesting is now the difference between the "peaks" of the two probability distributions, which in empirical frequency distributions would be the mean (MW_1 or MW_2). Since we are dealing with normal distributions, the difference values between the means must still be transformed or normalized into standard deviations, so that the so-called Z-values can be read from the relevant normal distribution tables, and the "discrimination index" (D′) can be formed according to the general formula:

$$D' = MW_1 - MW_2/SD \quad (SD = Standardabweichung)$$

$$\text{oder}: \quad D' = Z_1 - Z_2$$

Alternatively to the means from a study, frequency values or proportions can also be used to determine the Z-values from the probability table. In this case, it is assumed that the two normally distributed variables have one or the same standard deviations.

To estimate a test candidate's risk propensity in identifying signals, the "response tendency" or preference for hits or non-hits should also be determined in parallel to the discrimination index and related to each other according to the formula:

$$\text{Beta (R)} = \text{Anzahl Treffer/Anzahl Nicht} - \text{Treffer}$$

Beta (R) or β_R is also the decision criterion X_C, where the subject sets or marks their threshold in favor of one of the two decision alternatives. If the ratio of Beta > 1, the test subject tends to make more deliberate or cautious decisions and particularly keeps the number of non-hits (in the denominator) rather small. If they are more concerned with a high number of hit indications, the number of non-hits as "false alarms" inevitably increases, as the correct indication of hits (in the numerator) remains more or less the same or constant.

When scaling comparisons between two *different* variables or stimuli, which are to be judged, for example, as smaller vs. larger or equal vs. unequal, the measurement model changes, as the variances (and the standard deviation as a result of the square root of the variances) of both variables, even if they are the same size, must be considered. Thus, the formula for D′ in the operationalization of differences between two stimuli becomes:

$$D' = MW_A - MW_B/SD_{(MWA-MWB)} \times \sqrt{2}$$

Even before the conception of signal detection theory, the so-called "Thurstone scaling" was established in psychology as a scaling and measurement method based on the "method of paired comparison." In this procedure, *two* stimuli are also compared with each other on a chosen psychological quality or characteristic, such as equality or inequality. If the assumption is that the two stimuli or variables do not correlate with each other, the standard deviation also takes the form:

$$SD = \sqrt{SD_A^2 + SD_B^2} \quad \text{oder}: \quad \sqrt{2} \times \sqrt{SD_{A,B}^2} \quad \text{bzw.} \quad SD_{A,B} \times \sqrt{2}$$

7.3 Other Possibilities of System Diagnostics

$$\text{oder}: D' = MW_A - MW_B = Z_{p(A>B)} \times \sqrt{2}$$

as the so-called "pair comparison law".

7.3.1.2 Operationalization and Application

Studies on the recognition performance of certain signals (hits) or other stimuli (non-hits) require responses from the test subjects, such as correct or incorrect, or their agreement or rejection, and can be manipulated by means of an instruction of given frequencies or probabilities for the occurrence of a stimulus, e.g., by specifying: Variable A has an a priori probability of 70%, Variable B only 30%. To enable meaningful and representative evaluations, at least 100 trials should be planned. After completing the test runs, the frequency or proportion of hits and "false alarms", i.e., the proportion of non-hits among the yes-responses, is to be determined and their respective Z-values are to be taken from the normal distribution table (under the premise that the standard deviation is the same for both probability distributions).

Alternatively to signal detection as an experimental design, the specification of rating scales with a graduated scale (e.g., from 1 to 6 or as a percentage scale from 0%, 20%,… to 100%) for different degrees of agreement or rejection is also possible. Rating scales can then be evaluated according to a fixed procedure to determine the differences of interest between attitudes such as agreement or rejection (see e.g., Velden, 1982, p. 49).

In psychological research as well as in practice, the performance of the sensory systems was initially the focus and found the most frequent application. Of particular interest were studies on the perception threshold, i.e., from which frequency a certain tone is heard by the test subject with a certainty of at least 50% in all test rounds. Subjects were also exposed to consciously subliminal stimuli such as taboo words, which can trigger defense impulses, to explore the defense or reactance as sensitivity of the test subjects. According to current understanding, such stimuli should not become conscious but still influence the reactions. For example, tones were perceived worse when subliminal taboo words were simultaneously offered, which apparently disrupts and impairs the perception process sustainably.

Vigilance studies, which were or are also widespread in research and practice, test attention or concentration to perform a consistent continuous performance over a given period, or the vigilance decline due to fatigue or exhaustion.

Finally, in practice, tests on the truthfulness of statements or lies using lie detectors have become established, which contain both neutral items and critical items in connection with an event that only the perpetrator or the criminal investigators know. As with signal detection, the psychophysiological indicators are recorded as autonomous reactions of the suspect to the critical items and related to the total responses. Since the a priori probability of the critical crime-relevant items is known and given, an indicator as a clue or hint of a justified suspicion can be calculated from the formed relation between the anomalies or signals in critical items to the total number of item presentations. According to recent findings, the success rate for lie detectors, i.e., both identifying suspects and recognizing and excluding innocents as non-suspects, is 70% to 85% (see Schauer, 2022, p. 121 and Sect. 8.3).

7.3.2 Sampling or: "Setting an Example"

Some game theorists advocate the use of *unpredictability* (Dixit & Nalebuff, 1995, pp. 26 and 164 ff.) in moves as a strategy, which makes it difficult for the opponent to react adequately. A good example would be unplanned inspections or audits, which are abundant in "public life," such as mobile speed checks in traffic or unexpected customs inspections on construction sites or audits by tax authorities and social security agencies.

Even for regular taxpayers, the tax office can either conduct extensive audits and insist on proof of income or expenses to an unknown extent, or settle for sample checks, or even forgo them entirely in individual cases. For the "taxpayer," the behavior of the tax authorities is therefore unpredictable, and he (or she) must be prepared for all eventualities and adjust accordingly. Whether these actions have the character of strategic behavior or moves is debatable and at least contentious! Perhaps the following situation can provide clarity?

Assume the tax office is currently pursuing the "strategy" of thoroughly checking only one percent (1%) of tax returns, which, of course, the general public does not know, thereby keeping the audit and administrative effort as low as possible; it may be possible to define a ratio of effort to benefit as a "payoff" for this. Based on past experiences, approximately 20% of taxpayers attempted to evade or even avoid taxes, which in some cases and in severe offenses led to charges and the initiation of criminal proceedings (see Fig. 7.12). Thus, the tax office can only indirectly respond to the "tax morale" of taxpayers by varying the sample rate; a balance in the sense of game theory is unlikely given this initial situation.

The authors Dixit and Nalebuff (1995, pp. 164 ff.) have chosen playing tennis with a mixed strategy of alternating forehand and backhand serves by tennis players and illustrated it with their success rates as a payoff to illustrate the strategy of "unpredictability."

The designation of this "game": "Setting an Example" is intended to at least consider the deterrent effect for potential "tax evaders" when no one knows in advance whether they will be subject to an audit. Thus, the initial situation for this scenario is depicted in Fig. 7.12.

Rather than the outcome of a strategic game with an (inevitable) balance for both sides, this action is likely to be primarily based on an empirically determined result that depends significantly on chance. It is also doubtful whether the unchecked tax returns have an error rate of approximately 20%, as was repeatedly the case with the audited tax returns. Assumptions and conjectures thus replace strategic calculation when more emphasis is placed on the deterrent effect of unpredictability, i.e., will it affect me or not!

7.3 Other Possibilities of System Diagnostics

Person: A (lines)/ Tax office: B (columns)	Tax office checks (P = 1%)	Tax office does not check (1-P = 99%)	Marginal sum (lines)
Tax evasion (Yes - 20 %)	(P x N) x Yes (0.01 x 1000) x 0.20 = 2 (= hit)	(1 - P) x N x Yes (0.99 x 1000) x 0.20 198 (= dark figure)	200
Tax evasion (No = 80 %)	(P x N) x No (0.01 x 1000) x 0.80 = 8 (= False alarm)	(1 - P) x N x No Person: A 792 (= innocent)	800
Marginal total (columns)	10	990	N = 1000

Fig. 7.12 Payoff matrix for the case "Setting an Example"

It is easy to see that with a sample size or population of N = 1000 (taxpayers) and a rate of only 1% of audit cases, only a total of 10 tax returns are thoroughly and meticulously examined. With an assumed deception rate of 20%, the tax office would only catch two "tax evaders," and for eight taxpayers, there would be no significant objections (these would be the so-called "false alarms"). However, with an extrapolated or estimated "dark figure" of 198 tax evaders, the question arises for the future whether the low rate of 1% will remain or whether it should be increased to, for example, 5% or even 10% for a year to enhance the deterrent effect. Such a decision would indeed have strategic significance! Such a measure would also have the advantage of "shedding more light on the dark," i.e., illuminating the dark figure of tax evasion in the truest sense of the word and gaining better insights on a broader and more profound basis.

Presumably, the strategic approach in tax audits also lies in a sequentially oriented process or course of play, where none of the parties involved knows exactly what the other intends to do. In this context, the momentum of unpredictability would most likely be of particular importance, as taxpayers do not have even remotely (complete or imperfect) information about what the tax authorities plan and intend to do.

7.3.3 Portfolio Techniques for Self-Control and Self-Suggestion

So to speak, for self-suggestion, every organization should occasionally look in the mirror to see if it can be satisfied with its current performance and development status. In some cases, the individual assessment of people in responsible positions or as absolute specialists and "knowledge carriers" cannot be separated from a more comprehensive functional or system diagnostics. Nevertheless, the focus here is on the organizational units or functional areas and their procedural

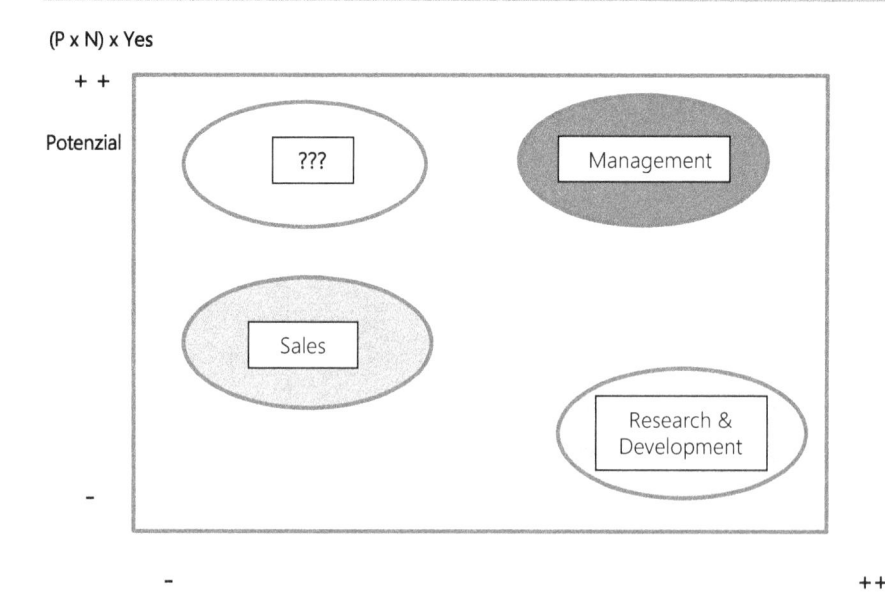

(P x N) x Yes

Fig. 7.13 Competence Portfolio "in one's own matter"

collaboration within the overall system. The result of this analysis could be presented in the form of a competence portfolio (see Fig. 7.13).

Personnel experts, as well as financial economists in particular, are of course sufficiently familiar with portfolio techniques as their most essential and decisive tool for strategic planning. What might be rather new or unusual is that not only foreign or other objects (or even subjects as in a personnel portfolio; see e.g. Wienkamp, 2020, p. 85 ff.) can be found in it, but that this tool is now to be used for self-control and one's own positioning in comparison to others. Of course, for example, the company management or the board should not be too proud to assess the business or product divisions as well as the supporting functional or operational areas according to defined strategic dimensions or quality factors within the framework of strategic planning and to derive targets for the future from this.

7.4 Summary

System diagnostics means nothing other than situational analyses of social relationships and their interactive processes against the background of strategic considerations and advantage calculations pursued by both competitors. Unlike personality or individual diagnostics, characters or personality profiles are not of interest in this type of analysis; rather, it is about the framework or "system rules" that the problem situation or a conflict thematically presents, such as the

7.4 Summary

regulation of damage between the "victim" and the damage causer, according to which both conflict parties must align themselves to best adapt their scope of action to the given alternatives. System diagnostics or system analysis is the simulation or "playing through" of potential decision-making and action possibilities with all their consequences.

Based on selected everyday scenarios, such as the aforementioned damage regulation or, for example, problems in collaboration in project work in working life, the critical influencing factors, which are closely linked to the interests and preferences of the involved actors, should be identified and analyzed and evaluated regarding their strategic relevance. Attention was also given to social psychological phenomena such as "Collective Non-Responsibility," which could explain the phenomenon of "failure to provide assistance," especially in the presence of several people, against the background of the absence or decrease of responsibility, e.g., to make an emergency call.

For certain situations, such as the detection of critical signals or errors, concepts for measurement and operationalization are available, which have been and are being applied in various psychological studies to assess the performance of "systems," such as the sensory system. A special case is the use of sampling procedures when it comes to the unpredictability of "system controls," such as in tax audits. For the self-control of functionalities, portfolio techniques are suitable, which inevitably exert suggestive influences on those responsible.

8 Economic Concepts of "Rational Decision-Making"

Unlike in the previous Chaps. 6 and 7 on game theory and its analyses as "system diagnostics," the economic models and procedures for rational decision-making do not recognize the interdependent or mutual influences through interactions of the participants, which massively influence decision-making. Nevertheless, there are substantive and methodological overlaps with game-theoretical approaches, for example, on the one hand, through the recourse to probability statements in the face of uncertainty about the occurrence of events or outcomes, and on the other hand, through the determination of expected utility, whose value or magnitude leads to the decision or selection to be favored among the offered alternatives. Also, in these procedural applications, there is talk of dominant and non-dominant alternatives, which are to be handled in the same way as game-theoretical strategies.

The starting situation in these models of rational decision-making is concrete but at first glance opaque problems with regard to the expected advantages and disadvantages, such as the selection of a new job among various offers, which are to be optimally or best solved in accordance with the individual preference structure and taking into account expected risks or uncertainties. In other words: It is not the utility maximization that arises depending on the reactions of a competing counterparty that is the "show stage" of the expected utility theory, but rather it is about the utility maximization that most closely aligns with one's own ideas and preferences regarding the offered alternatives!

8.1 Theoretical Concept and Methodological Implications

The following basic model should be considered in the theory of expected utility (see, e.g., Eisenführ et al., 2010, pp. 20 ff.):

"1) Action alternatives: A decision problem always involves a choice among different alternatives, which are characterized as a 'profile' by differently pronounced or even existing attributes.
2) Environmental influences: Environmental or situational influences at least *indirectly* flow into decision-making, as the decision-maker cannot directly influence them and is inevitably exposed to them (this is also, as mentioned several times, the essential difference from game theory in the person of the co-player and his or her influencing decisions). At most, he includes them in his considerations through expectations or probability statements.
3) Consequences: True to the principle advocated here, "One cannot *not* manipulate!" no one can make decisions or react without it having consequences. Depending on the considered decision alternatives and their possible impacts on the situation or environment, certain consequences arise, which are either advantageous or disadvantageous for the decision-maker.
4) Goals and preferences: To be able to speak of advantages or disadvantages at all, a goal determination or a preference structure is required, which determines what is particularly important in this decision and its expected impacts. Individual goals and preferences are thus the basis for an optimal decision among several alternatives as offers."

It should not go unmentioned that the search for alternative possibilities can also be a laborious endeavor, which in the end may not necessarily be crowned with success and may not completely satisfy those affected. For example, one might think of the search for the new "ideal" job holder for a vacant position, where perhaps after numerous interviews with applicants, no satisfactory solution has yet been found.

But candidates can also struggle when they are presented with multiple job offers and have more "the agony than the choice," as the job profiles differ significantly in important criteria. It is not only the salary levels that matter, but also the development opportunities or career prospects are a decisive factor for the future. Many applicants pay attention to the "work-life balance" (see Wienkamp, 2023c, pp. 75 ff.), so that working time regulations (e.g., "4-day week") or the location, such as a big city or university town with plenty of cultural leisure activities, or also the type or size of the organization as a new employer become important decision criteria.

With too much effort, it should not be surprising that people eventually give up trying to solve their problem analytically-rationally and instead decide "from the gut," following their intuition or an inspiration. Intuitive decisions do not necessarily have to be wrong and can ultimately make the difference despite all the analysis and rationality. It is not without reason that psychology has taken up the study of intuitive decision-making and has contributed very important findings in the context of the so-called "Descriptive or Cognitive Decision Theory" (see, e.g., Kahneman, 2011).

Attempts at manipulation have nothing in common with rational decision procedures, where the actors pretend to want to decide and act according to rational or reasonable criteria, but in reality, are only looking for a "cloak" to disguise or hide their already fixed intentions. In such "games," the end result is predetermined, according to personal preferences or a politically oriented interest position, and it is only pretended that analysis, selection, and decision-making are based on objective criteria. This type of decision-making is often observed in groups with political decision-making calculations, where one or more manipulators "pull the strings" in the background until the desired collective result "is on the table." One might think of the selection of the venue for international sporting events such as the Football World Cup or the Olympic Games, which are predestined as examples and where sometimes criminal activities through the use of bribes have been alleged or generally cannot be ruled out as manipulation maneuvers.

Personnel decisions can similarly be "cooked up" through hidden secret agreements or coalition formations and have been part of the political business of the powerful and decision-makers since time immemorial.

8.2 Application Example

To get out of this decision dilemma and solve the selection problem, the authors Eisenführ et al. (2010, p. 109 ff.) prepared a scenario where a "newly minted" university graduate, after passing his exams, sought a first job and had to choose among several offers. Based on the decision path outlined here, the application of the expected utility theory could be excellently demonstrated in all procedural sections and with the most important evaluation methods (to give the reader the opportunity to follow or deepen the present calculations and explanations, the alternatives with their numerical data from the specified source were not changed and were adopted as such). The following offers were available for selection in this example (see Eisenführ et al., 2010, p. 139):

"1) Entry into a management consultancy with an annual salary of €80,000, approximately 60 hours of work per week, and "good" career prospects;
2) Assistant or doctoral position at a university with a salary of €50,000, 40 hours of work, and "excellent" career prospects;
3) initially working as a sailing instructor with a salary of €30,000, 20 hours of work, and "poor" or no career prospects."

For the university graduate, the decision did not seem easy, so on the recommendation of a former fellow student, he decided to transfer the job offers with their feature profiles into a "value function" to a) weight (or normalize) the attributes of the positions and b) make them comparable to arrive at a well-founded decision.

According to this procedure, the decision-maker forms an evaluation interval from *Minimum* to *Maximum* (or poor to very good). Thus, the worst feature expression always receives the value zero (0) and the best always 1.0 (or also 100%). For the salary, for example, the following interval results: €80,000 = 1.0 as maximum; €30,000 = 0 as minimum. For the intermediate feature values, a value factor is to be found by interpolation if a freely selectable function course from 0 to 1.0 is assumed. Using the *"method of equal value differences"*, the interpolation could, for example, be implemented so that the following result is obtained:

"1) (€30,000:€40,000) is equivalent to (€40,000: "?")
2) since the difference of €40,000 − €30,000 = €10,000
3) and the ratio or result of €10,000:€40,000 = 0.25 is,
4) the sought threshold value (?) should have the same relation of 0.25; thus, at €40,000:0.75 = €53,333, the upper threshold value would correspond to the median (= 0.50) of this value function."

For the hours of work volume, the value structure is comparatively simple if 60 hours as the most negative expression receives the value zero, a working time of 20 hours the maximum value of 1.0, and the working time of 40 hours per week, which lies exactly in the middle, also takes the middle in the value function with 0.5.

In the next final step, it is about the comparability of different features with their expressions in the course of a multiple approach. Various methods are available for this, such as the *"trade-off method"* as a frequently used method for determining *equivalents* or subjectively perceived indifferences between two attributes offered for comparison. The corresponding comparison values of a feature are sought, which are indifferent, i.e., equivalent, for the evaluator in view of another combination of these features.

"1) If we try to compare the working time with the best value = 20 hours for the sailing instructor and the worst value of 60 hours in management consulting with the salaries for equivalence, we form this approach:

20 hours–60 hours: "?" – €30,000

2) Assuming the respondent would decide on €55,000 as an equivalent after several comparison rounds, then the approach for determining weights would result (see Eisenführ et al., 2010, p. 141):

20 hours–60 hours:€55,000 – €30,000 = 1:0.7 = 1.429

(the divisor of 0.7 corresponds to the normalized value in the course of an exponential function on the basis (e $^{-x}$) for the salary of €55,000)"

The above-mentioned result from the comparison of working time on the one hand and salary on the other is the mathematically resulting "reciprocal" of the relation of working time to salary in the amount of €55,000 (and can possibly also be used for further comparison calculations).

For the final comparison of the offered positions based on the value assessments for the selected and relevant characteristic expressions, however, the decision criteria were taken from the value function. They are for the *consulting:* Salary = 1.0, Working hours = 0, and Career prospects = 0.7 (as a qualitative assessment); for the *university:* Salary = 0.6, Working hours = 0.5, and Career prospects = 1.0; and for the job as a *sailing instructor:* Salary = 0, Working hours = 1.0, and Career prospects = 0.

A summation of the weights from the value function with subsequent normalization based on their total sum would lead to the following share (in %) of the weight factors of these characteristics, such as Salary: 1.0 (at 80 T€) + 0.7 (at 55 T€) + 0.91 (at 70 T€) = 2.61 (the salary equivalent of 70 T€ was derived, by the way, from the comparison Salary : Career prospects).

Then the influence of the attribute Salary would be, for example, measured at the total weight 1:2.61 = 0.38 (or 38%) in terms of "salary equivalents" for all three characteristics as a common comparison size. For the remaining characteristics Working hours and Career prospects, the influence on weight (in percentage values) is also to be determined according to this scheme. It is 0.27 (27%) for Working hours and 0.35 (35%) for Career prospects.

By multiplying the weight share (e.g., 0.38) and the preference value of the characteristic in the value function, the final result for the decision of a job is obtained after summation. Thus, for example, according to this procedure, the offer from the university would be the most lucrative and prevail in the evaluation and selection; or in numbers:

> "0.38 × 0.6 (value preference for university salary) + 0.27 × 0.5 (value preference for working hours) + 0.35 × 1.0 (value preference for the best career prospects) = 0.71.
>
> The consulting firm would achieve a total benefit of 0.63 and the position as a sailing instructor of 0.27, thus clearly lying below the result of the university in this comparison."

A similar but more extensive example is the case study by Düsch (2001, p. 1 ff.), which deals with the selection of a foreign language education either as a future translator or interpreter and illustrated this path in a multi-stage process with comparatively more offers and a more extensive "colorful" characteristic profile. Other alternative case studies applied the much more complex methods of the *multi-attribute utility theory* to evaluate and compare completely different decision problems with different, alternative objectives, such as the establishment of more training positions for one's own talent development and demand coverage versus no or reduced in-company training and instead more external hiring of already qualified personnel (e.g., Kastner, 2001, p. 89 ff.).

8.3 Other Remarks

With the expected utility theory, there is a theory about "rational decision-making itself," because it holds either expected value (Alternative A) > expected value (Alternative B) for a positive decision for A or expected value (Alternative A) = expected value (Alternative B) in case of indifference or equality of the alternatives. With the help of "procedural rationality" (Eisenführ et al., 2010, p. 5 ff.), this procedure is intended to prevent an arbitrary decision. Non-arbitrariness is thus the "trademark" of prescriptive procedures.

In many application cases, there are knowledge or information gaps, or the events are simply random variables that cannot be determined deterministically but can only be statistically calculated or better delineated using probability expectations. When operating with probability statements, the pending comparison is either, on the one hand, an alternative with a certain result, such as a guaranteed profit or payout, or, on the other hand, an alternative with a higher profit prospect, however, not guaranteed at 100%, but only as a "lottery" with a probability indication for the potential success or profit.

Sometimes the notions of the occurrence of an event are very vague and imprecise, for example, when speaking of "rarely," "sometimes," or "almost always." The probability concept could thus also fall under the so-called "indeterminate legal terms," which are usually to be defined and specified in each individual case. For the side effects of medications, for example, the regulatory authorities have therefore provided these adjectives with concrete specifications, i.e., with frequency intervals, so that any layperson can understand them (see Eisenführ et al., 2010, p. 182).

Among the most well-known calculation methods based on probabilities is the so-called "Bayes' Theorem," which, for example, Eisenführ et al. (2010, pp. 194 ff.) developed and presented for the application of a lie detector test. Based on the initial situation, the following expectations (marked as probability indications with the expression p) are to be assumed (the numerical data were also adopted):

"1) A-priori probabilities: p (for guilty) = 0.7; p (for innocent) = 0.3
2) The conditional probabilities (or likelihoods):

p (Test pos./Guilty) = 0.9; p (Test pos./Innocent) = 0.2
p (Test neg./Guilty) = 0.1; p (Test neg./Innocent) = 0.8

3) Calculation of the joint probability:

p (Guilty, and Test neg.) = p (Guilty) × p (Test neg., but guilty)
p = 0.7 × 0.1 = 0.07

4) Calculation of the probability that the test is negative: p (Test neg.)

= p (Guilty) × p (Test neg./Guilty) + p (Innocent) × p (Test neg./Innocent)
= 0.7 × 0.1 + 0.3 × 0.8 = 0.31

5) Calculation of the a-posteriori probabilities, once

a) p (Guilty/Test neg.) => p (Guilty/Test neg.): p (Test neg.)
p = 0.07:0.31 = 0.226
b) p (Guilty/Test pos.) =>
p (Guilty) × p (Guilty/Test pos.): p (Guilty) × p (Guilty/Test pos.) +
p (Innocent) × p (Innocent/Test pos.)
p = 0.7 × 0.9 (0.7 × 0.9 + 0.3 × 0.2) = 0.913"

According to the Bayes approach, the *a-priori* probabilities initially exist as basic probabilities for a specific event, which are the first to be included in the calculation. In this example, these would be the basic probability for "guilty" or "innocent." Based on the given test statistics, probabilities about the quality of the test are available, indicating how well the test can correctly (or incorrectly) diagnose the present cases. An important test criterion is the "false alarms" as an error rate when the test shows a positive result (e.g., guilty) that does not apply (that would be test positive, but innocent). In the next step, the *joint* probabilities from a-priori probabilities and test statistics are of interest, which result from multiplication and are then weighted, i.e., divided by the total sum over all alternatives. This result would then be the *a-posteriori* probability, which is a final result of this calculation (see also the scheme by Eisenführ et al., 2010, p. 200).

Perhaps a word about the probabilities a-priori probability and a-posteriori probability. Binmore (2009, p. 127) defined these probability sizes as follows: "Your prior probabilities quantify your beliefs before something happens. Your posterior probabilities quantify after it has happened." A-priori probabilities can thus be both objective probability calculations based on a statistical evaluation of an event in a population (e.g., the frequency or probability of women or men succumbing to a particular disease) and subjective probability estimates that correspond to one's personal experience horizon and are used as input in the Bayes' Theorem. The purpose and advantage of the Bayes approach is to start with an estimated probability, e.g., according to "gut feeling," and successively incorporate new information (as "updating") into the calculation until the a-priori probability becomes a consistent and reliable calculation size based on profound and stable experiences. Thus, the a-posteriori probabilities also gain increasing significance and become more realistic in their predictions (see Binmore, 2009, pp. 126 ff.).

A special variant for obtaining a priori probabilities was introduced by Raiffa (1970, p. 28) when a decision-maker is given the opportunity to purchase or view the a priori probability distribution of an attribute or criterion in a defined population group for a certain amount (e.g., a fee), or is allowed to draw a specific sample from the population group and determine the probability. As further shown, the expenditure must naturally be considered as a cost in the utility calculation and deducted from the average expected profit. In the end, however, the expenditure can be worthwhile, as on the one hand, the expected values can be calculated more accurately, and on the other hand, due to the knowledge and the resulting decision, a profit is more likely than a loss.

Test diagnostics using the Bayes method have, with the exception of the calculation of a posteriori probabilities, many similarities with the already presented signal detection theory (see Sect. 7.3.1). However, the Bayes approach methodologically goes beyond the investigations (or diagnostics) of signal detection theory.

It should be noted, however, that especially in medical screening for the early detection of malignant diseases, such as tumors through mammograms or other early detection methods, it is not only the test statistics with their important parameters "sensitivity" and "specificity" that matter (see already section 7.3.1), but also the a priori probabilities for the respective cancer or tumor disease must be considered in planning the next steps of investigation, especially since most early detection methods do not test and diagnose without error rates and are absolutely reliable and safe. Only the low a posteriori probabilities can provide a certain degree of hope and confidence that there may not be a malignant disease after all, even if they cannot completely reassure patients about their current health status, as a residual risk remains.

It is not by chance that the impression might arise that evaluation procedures for searching and selecting a "best" decision suggest a disciplined approach in methodology. Self-discipline is neither out of place nor suboptimal; on the contrary, it is the guarantee for correct evaluations and solutions when applying the expected utility theory. At the same time, the methodology or "the system" exerts an immediate compulsion to adhere to the rules, which presupposes a natural willingness and a certain degree of self-suggestion to motivate oneself for it.

8.4 Summary

In presenting the model of expected utility theory, the natural question certainly arose as to what this procedure has to do with the diagnostics of manipulations. As already explained, it is the self- or autosuggestion to follow a predetermined (meaningful) path and to absolutely maintain the course once taken.

Unlike perhaps other alternative decision models, expected utility theory attempts to fully, or as best as possible, correspond to rational or reasonable thinking and acting. The prerequisite for this is the strict adherence to "procedural rationality" (see above), i.e., self-disciplined rule-compliant behavior. All calculated and thus proposed results are deeply "rational" and consistent in terms of the applied methodology—and far removed from any arbitrary influence.

Whether, however, risk potentials could arise in fundamental strategic thinking is a completely different question, which may only be answered using completely different perspectives and concepts than those presented here.

Calculating or perhaps "juggling" with probability assumptions can be both a "curse and a blessing." On the one hand, probability values are always an expression of uncertainty about the occurrence of an event and thus dependent on and shaped by chance; on the other hand, probability statements can also provide hope if, after a screening, there is only a low risk (i.e., only a low probability suggests) of developing a malignant cancer or similar.

Insights into the Influence on Prosocial Behavior

9

With the available arsenal of games, there was a "toolbox" (see Chaps. 6 and 7), which, with its game versions, stimulated and enabled a wealth of experimental investigations into both selfish-rational thinking and behavior, as well as, in addition, prosocial behavior. Even neuroeconomics (see, for example, the anthology by Gilmcher et al., 2009), which as a "research community" mainly dealt with studies on decision problems in specific situations, frequently used games as a research design for this purpose. In addition, the researchers determined the neurophysiological resonance in the decision-makers through activity measurements in the respective relevant brain regions using magnetic resonance imaging (English: functional magnetic resonance imaging or fMRI).

In most experimental investigations, two subjects faced each other as players when they engaged in, for example, the already introduced ultimatum game or the dictator game (see Sect. 6.2.2.2). A parameter for brain activity in such games is the oxygen content in the blood, which is defined and known as "Blood Oxygen Level Dependent" or abbreviated as "BOLD signal."

In the dictator game, as is well known, one player makes a (supposedly) fair distribution proposal, on which the other player has no influence. In the relevant experiments, observers as test subjects, who were subjected to neurophysiological measurements with the fMRI, then assessed the degree of perceived fairness with either positive or negative reactions. In this research design, the two players are merely "actors" and not the subjects to be examined, as these are the observers.

It is different in the ultimatum game, where, following the preceding distribution proposal of one player, the other player makes the decision for themselves whether to accept the proposal because they consider it fair from their perspective or not. In this case, the second player, as the decision-maker, must undergo a magnetic resonance imaging to measure their brain activity as a correlate or as a supplement to their emotional state, which would be determined through a subsequent survey.

Prosocial behavior, as understood here, depends very much on one's own social preferences and the understanding and empathy (i.e., the empathy shown) for the current and personal situation of fellow human beings.

9.1 Social Preferences in the Assessment of Interactions

So far, decisions or behavior resulting from selfish motives have dominated economic models, which also led to plausible statements under competitive conditions and in situations of competition. A typical example of this type is the well-known *Homo oeconomicus*, who is also assumed to have pronounced rationality in thinking and acting (see Chap. 8). However, as soon as strategic thinking and acting are required and appear necessary, the reactions of other people can gain great game-determining significance, so that the involved actors align their strategies according to their "social preferences." Social preferences are then the individual positive or negative consequences of one's own actions on the people affected by them. Thus, as soon as an individual takes responsibility for the well-being of other people, he (or she) is influenced and guided by social preferences. Fairness and social reciprocity become the decisive values and criteria for assessing the behavior of other people in social contexts. Good examples of social preferences are helpfulness and willingness to donate to charitable causes. Strategic calculations do not mean unconditionally submitting to the wishes and sensitivities of others and ignoring one's own advantage, e.g., as the difference between costs and returns (or generally utility).

With the research designs from game theory for analyzing interactive and interdependent actions, such as in the context of the ultimatum or dictator game, these social-psychological factors like fairness, trust, sense of justice, altruism, and social reciprocity, with or without judging and possibly sanctioning spectators, could be examined. Impressive effects were found, for example, in the examination of fair behavior. For instance, unfair behavior did not occur when some participants anticipated negative consequences for their own possible unfair behavior, while another part was only willing to engage in "fair play" after being sanctioned or punished for their unfair behavior. Similarly, the degree of fairness in the ultimatum game among players (or in the presence of observers) was significantly greater than in the dictator game, which per se does not foresee or exclude reciprocal reactions like punishment or revenge. Thus, the rate of "fairness" as a criterion in the dictator game was between 10% and 20%, while the proportion in the other game variant (ultimatum game) ranged between 30% and 60% (see Fehr, 2009, p. 220).

Furthermore, neurophysiological studies have shown that the reaction to, for example, unfair offers strongly correlated with activity in certain brain areas, which also indicated a corresponding emotionalization of the test subjects (such as indignation or anger). As soon as self-serving motives in terms of rewards ("Social Rewards") were served, brain activity possibly shifted to other brain areas. This was also true when compliance with current social norms was shown out of self-interest to avoid unpleasant reactions.

9.2 Compassion (Empathy) with Other People

In social interactions, not only judgments about people and their behavior are predominant and of interest. Social factors or personality traits that shape and influence social interaction or action, or the social climate from within, i.e., from the personality structure and the psychological experience of those involved, are equally of interest.

Of great importance is the "social or emotional understanding," as I would call it, which means, on the one hand, becoming clear about what drives or motivates the other person at the moment, what thoughts they are pursuing about the current situation or the mutual relationship, and what reactions are to be expected and how the other can adjust to it. Models of social cognition refer to this process as "mind-reading" or simply call it the "theory of mind." On the other hand, it is about emotional participation in the life or fate of another person and, in particular, their feelings, to put oneself quite accurately in their situation and understand them emotionally, which can be described as empathy.

Empathy, alongside the already mentioned social preferences, is the essential prerequisite for help or other support services, such as donations or acts of charity, and only functions when the emotional states of the two people in relation strongly converge or run synchronously and overlap. Emotional pain, such as grief or similar, that the other person is currently experiencing and suffering from, is conveyed through compassion as "our pain," which we then feel and perceive somewhere in our body.

Social influences thus occur both on the cognitive level through the anticipated thoughts and intentions and on the emotional track through compassion, as the other person infects us with their current experience, making us more or less consciously aware of it involuntarily. According to neuropsychology findings, mirror neurons seem to be responsible for the emergence or understanding of social cognition, which cause the imitation of movements and behavior of others (see Singer, 2009, p. 254 ff.). Whether mirror neurons also allow for the empathy of abstract mental processes such as thoughts or beliefs, as well as feelings, initially remained open, largely due to inadequate and unspecific research conditions, such as film screenings, photos with emotional facial expressions of people, etc. It was most possible to empathize with the applied and perceived pain of the target person. The same brain regions were active in both the target person and the observers. It should also be noted that the sensations occurred automatically and without explicit instruction in the experiments, such as during a film screening (see Singer, 2009, p. 257 ff.).

Questionnaire surveys also showed that there are differential differences in empathy between people, which even positively correlated with neurophysiological measurements. In the German-speaking area, the test by Leibetseder et al. (2001) is known as the "Empathy Scale."

In general, it can be assumed that fairness and empathy occupy the largest part of what is understood as prosocial behavior. In games, fairness was or is a condition for cooperation, where non-cooperation or unfairness is gladly punished "with pleasure" and is indicated as enjoyment or reward neuropsychologically in the images taken. Naturally, empathy also promotes cooperative behavior, as empathy prevents harm to others and corresponds to what religion roughly understands as "charity."

Occasionally, it can happen that empathetic reactions are replaced or overlaid by desires for revenge or "schadenfreude" when others experience bad things or have bad experiences for one's own satisfaction.

9.3 Summary

Not only self-interest is simultaneously a driver and "transmission belt" for social influences, but social preferences and the compassion felt also give rise to impulses for prosocial behavior. Prosocial actions, similar to rational behavior, are subject to important personal goals or concerns and therefore necessarily take on strategic traits or forms.

Disruptions in interactions can quickly occur, as findings from games used to investigate them showed, when the prevailing social norms of fairness and social reciprocity are violated. Emotional reactions are shown not only verbally, if applicable, but also through specific patterns of arousal or activity in the brain.

Implications and Consequences for Practice 10

Looking back, it should be acknowledged and noted that psychodiagnostics addresses and is active in two different fields of application or areas of investigation. On the one hand, in the classical manner of personality diagnostics of individual persons, and on the other hand, in situational and interpersonal or collective events and processes, each of which has its own "rules of the game" and influences the course of events. Common to all these observable occurrences are the social interactions, which, if you will, take place "on an open stage" and must be sought and analyzed in their specific niche.

10.1 Overview of the Structure of Social Interactions

The accompanying Fig. 10.1 is intended to provide an initial overview of the overall situation of relevant social interactions and to highlight the most important applications in practice in the further course.

As a basic structure, the relationship level and the communication level initially function, which are then expanded by further functionalities, such as consultations, negotiations, and interrogations, and extend to the operational and content level (or factual level).

Apart from conversations for general entertainment (i.e., chats) or for the purpose of normal news or information exchange (e.g., "How is the weather today?" or "Is the train delayed today?"), social interactions among people take place in some communicative manner, i.e., usually verbally (but also non-verbally), to achieve certain action goals. Since it is impossible to "not *not*communicate" (according to Watzlawick et al., 1982), it is equally impossible to "not *not* manipulate" (see already Sect. 1.2)! Both in all their diversity on the communication level and on the relationship level, social interactions or interpersonal processes are noticeable and observable. Depending on the field of application, such as financial

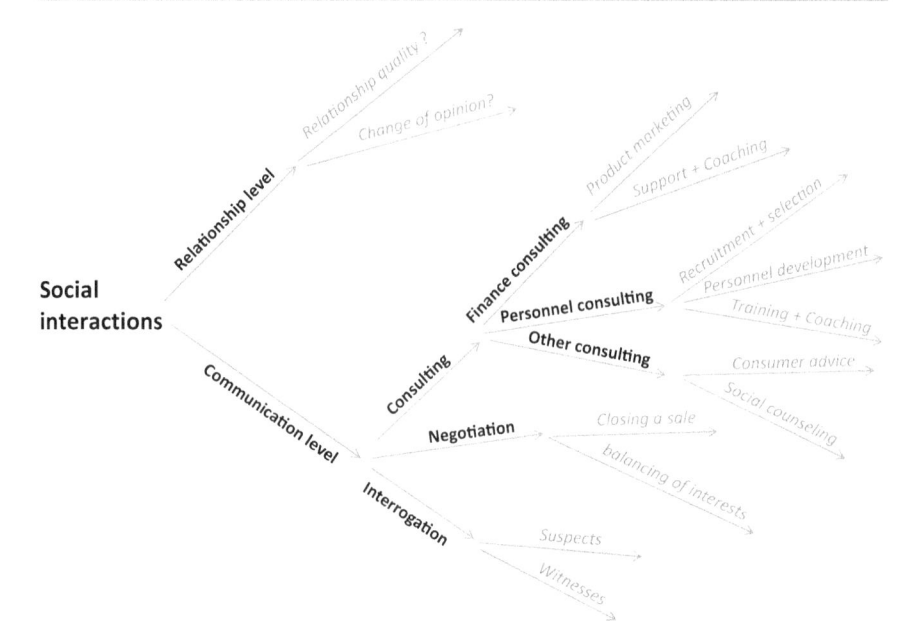

Fig. 10.1 Overview of the structure and course of social interactions

consulting, the tasks or behavioral intentions can then be specified as "business purposes" (marked in red in Fig. 10.1).

As already mentioned and emphasized in many communication models, communication includes both the interpersonal relationship with all psychological influences or imponderables and the content-related or subject- or object-related communication, which is responsible for the transformation of information.

10.2 Relationship Level

Fritz Heider (1958) was the first to extensively address the influence on relationships as a result of social interactions (or communication) in the past. His "Balance Theory," which emerged from his research activities, is still considered by today's social psychologists to be both "up to date" and simple and convincing (see, for example, Crandell et al., 2007). According to this model, which is based on a general "common sense," all social or interpersonal communication processes strive for a state of balance or equilibrium. If this balance is disturbed and thrown "off balance" by, for example, disagreements or differing assessments of situations, manipulative actions occur to restore the balance. In these social or communicative processes, both the individual opinion formation on a specific topic or object (which can also be a target person) and the relationship between the two interlocutors are relevant and affected (as depicted in Fig. 10.1 by the two branches "Relationship Quality?" and "Opinion Change?").

10.2 Relationship Level

In contrast to general communication models, which also assume a relationship level and a content or factual level, Heider represented the communicative processes between two people (referred to here as Peter and Paul) and an object as a "triangular relationship" (Wienkamp, 2022b, p. 94), as expressed in Fig. 10.2.

Depending on the initial situation, every form of social interaction or communication, whether as a discussion, disagreement, etc., always impacts the quality of the relationship, with the consequence that the actors try everything to restore a balance between the personal assessment of the interlocutor and the opinion content, thereby optimally influencing their own inherent processes. Balance is synonymous with harmony and equilibrium and stabilizes or reinforces one's self-concept. Generally speaking, this means "a person is at peace with themselves" when this state is achieved. The situational constellations depicted in Fig. 10.3 are to be assumed within the framework of Balance Theory.

As can be seen from these five illustrations, the first (upper) three relationship and opinion patterns are in balance (see Fig. 10.3), whereas the latter two (lower) are not, but are in imbalance. A balance is achieved when all (three) relationships are positive (+) or when one relationship side or connection is positive (+) and two are negative (−). This means nothing other than that, on the one hand, both the relationship quality between the two interlocutors and their opinion on a given topic agree and are positively valued. On the other hand, either the two people may not like each other and find that they have differing opinions, which corresponds to their "worldview," or their relationship with each other is positive or good, and they find that they both have a negative attitude or opinion on a topic or object, which also means harmony.

A disturbance of the balance or this "harmony triangle," as it could also be called, immediately leads to manipulative reactions either towards the interlocutor

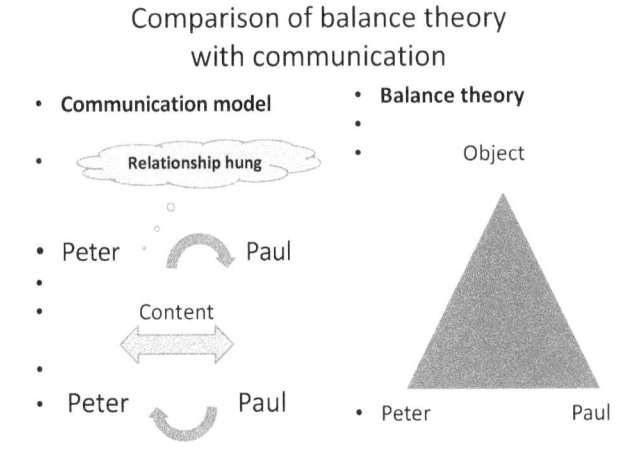

Fig. 10.2 Comparison of Balance Theory with Communication. (From Wienkamp, 2022b, p. 95)

Fig. 10.3 Constellations of Interpersonal Relationships. (From Wienkamp, 2022b, p. 96)

Constellations of interpersonal relationships

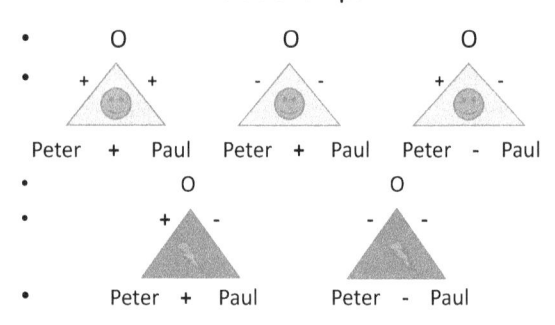

as attempts at persuasion or conviction or to self-manipulation, which concerns either one's own opinion or the existing "cognitive (evaluation) schemas" or one's self-image, to bring about a change. However, the attitude towards the other person can also change, from, for example, an originally sympathetic to now rather unsympathetic impression, etc., which also changes the quality of the interpersonal relationship.

10.3 Communication Level

Of the many or even countless communicative encounters, only the three variants a) consultation, b) negotiation, and c) interrogation will be particularly appreciated and discussed in this context from the perspective of social influences.

10.3.1 Consultation

With consulting, the most complex application area of communication is addressed at the same time. In addition to consulting to support other people through, for example, non-binding advice, recommendations, or suggestions offered without personal interests, there are also self-serving interventions or consulting services aimed at fulfilling a specific purpose. These include, for example, all consulting activities within the framework of a supervisory relationship, such as in sports by a coach who is also interested, for selfish reasons, in ensuring that his or her "protégé" delivers the desired and expected performances in competitions and, for example, comes home with a medal. The same applies to all types of educational tasks, whether in the family, at school, or in vocational training, where more or less clearly with instructions or, in a softened manner, with recommendations, operations are conducted, and, if you will, manipulation occurs.

Particularly sensitive to attempts at social influence are, on the one hand, financial consulting, where it ultimately concerns "one's own money," and on the other hand, personnel consulting in the broadest sense, namely from personnel search and selection to coaching, which includes both personality development and the practice or training of certain skills or techniques. Finally, as representatives of other consulting activities, public institutions as consumer consulting and social consulting (e.g., as debt counseling centers) should be mentioned, which provide special care through their consulting and support services to ordinary consumers or people in emergency situations.

10.3.1.1 Financial Consulting

Financial consulting is actually a form of consulting where, as lawyers put it, it is about "good faith." Trust in the suggestions, recommendations, or financial offers is indeed required and unavoidable on the one hand, but on the other hand, it is burdened with possible or even significant risks for the financial consumer if the financial advisor focuses more on marketing his financial products than on the real needs of his client.

In addition to the pure product brokerage (or better, sales) on a commission basis, as the financing and investment business is conducted by financial advisors or customer service representatives at banks and savings banks or by the field service of insurance companies or building societies (not to mention and quite apart from "structured sales"), independent fee-based advisors also offer their services for a fixed fee. They do not accept commissions from product providers per se, and the financial offers and their producers are selected at their own discretion, i.e., according to their own quality criteria for the respective suitable consumer group. Should commissions from providers flow during business mediation, they would pass them on to their clients as a sign of their independence and credibility.

The primary focus of financial advisors should be the needs assessment of the financial customer, which is directed a) according to his asset and income situation, b) according to his financial goals or plans, and c) according to his financial resilience ("risk-bearing capacity"), which can vary significantly from person to person depending on the consumer or financial type. Financial resilience depends not only on financial goals or customer wishes, such as financing a property or building a private pension, but also consumption habits and the propensity to save are essential influencing factors that must be considered.

Specially trained "psycho-specialists" are required to get a picture of the client's "financial personality" (see Wienkamp, 2019, p. 105 ff.) with all their individual preferences, inclinations, and fantasies, as well as the prevailing attitudes and personality traits regarding financial matters (such as risk tendencies). That would be the "nonplusultra" of insights! Seen in this way, "financial coaches" primarily engage with the client's personality and try to get to know him (or her) more precisely in financial dispositions and to help and support him (or her) in his (or her) decisions. Occasionally, these experts may encounter unexpected, hidden personality problems in dealing with financial matters ("money disorders"; see, for example, Canale et al., 2015, p. 35 ff.), which require deep psychological therapy by a psychotherapist familiar with this issue (see also Chap. 11).

In financial consulting, and especially in product marketing, one must assume different levels of knowledge (this is the asymmetric information distribution or supply, as it is called and problematized in professional circles), which inevitably serve as a breeding ground for manipulation attempts to the advantage of the customer advisor. Later, these disadvantageous contract conclusions can cause significant conflict material if, for example, the customer cannot get out of these "onerous contracts" or only by accepting significant financial losses, such as when high cancellation fees are charged.

On the other hand, it involves the investment of trust in the consulting competence and seriousness of the financial advisor, which is ultimately not easily discernible for the financial consumer. Therefore, the customer should and must conduct careful preparation with the analysis of all conceivable risks in his own interest before this consulting appointment. Above all, this includes the courage in the later consultation conversation to repeatedly ask the financial advisor about unknown technical terms or incomprehensible processes or results!

To be well-prepared for this, the financial client should anticipate some possible manipulation maneuvers or conversation techniques of the advisor and carefully plan their reactions. Additionally, during preparation, the person should also ask themselves, what kind of "financial personality" am I, for example, a risk-affine or risk-averse type, and where could my "blind spots" or other "handicaps" (or in extreme cases, the "money disorders") in financial matters lie, which the advisor might detect, recognize, and exploit during the consultation? A relatively methodically secured self-analysis based on a short test with the characteristics *incentive motivation* for reward sensitivity (or here the pursuit of profit and return) and *risk tolerance* in risky decisions (see e.g., Wienkamp, 2019, pp. 268 ff.) can be very helpful and provide initial clues and insights about the so-called "financial decision-maker."

Regardless of one's own preparation for financial advisory discussions, it should not be forgotten that the legislator, here the European Commission and the supervisory authorities commissioned by it, have also issued binding regulations or guidelines on investment and financial transactions. Thus, in principle, every financial advisor is obliged, within the framework of needs assessment (see above), to determine the *"suitability"* of the available financial products for the potential interested party by specifically inquiring about the financial plans (needs), the financial circumstances, and the determination of the individual *risk appetite* as a subjective attitude or personality trait before considering specific product offers and their sale or mediation. If the financial consumer provides no or only vague information on this, no sale of financial or investment products may be conducted, and the consultation would (actually) be over.

What exactly is meant by risk appetite and how this characteristic is to be operationalized or diagnosed, the legislator has not commented on, leaving a "design gap" for banks and financial advisors. Besides some "hand-knitted" tests on risk inclination and "money management" by financial advisors in the English-speaking world (see Wienkamp, 2019, pp. 266 f.), only the standardized instruments such as the *"FinaMetrica Risk Tolerance Test"* (see e.g., the contribution by Davey & Resnik, 2009, pp. 94 ff. or on the internet at: www.riskprofiling.com) and the *"Six & Six – Personality Test on Your Business and Financial Profile"* (Wienkamp, in prep.) are available.

Additionally, it should be absolutely clear to the financial consumer that, with the exception of loans or credits with a fixed term and interest rate or capital life insurance with guaranteed interest, financial offers are promises, or better, "uncovered checks" on the future, as no one in this world can accurately foresee the future development of financial markets. All parameters such as average *return* or *volatility* as a range of fluctuation for the possible risk are based on past data and developments. In all investment transactions, whether stocks, bonds, or funds, the return expectations sometimes depend on "colleague chance" (i.e., market fluctuations), which is always a risk, and any potential benefit only reveals itself later—if at all!

It is known from the relevant trade press that many customer advisors like to conceal possible investment risks from their clients, distract from them ("defocus"), or "de-dramatize" them. Furthermore, their conversation strategy is designed to always be "two steps ahead" of their conversation partners, to guide them or steer the conversation in a certain direction, which is nothing other than manipulation. Starting with the opening question (which is often embedded in an apparent request, i.e., for permission to ask questions about the person at all), the "show" begins as the prelude to a conscious and intentional influence with: "May I ask you a few personal questions?" to which the client casually and naturally says "Yes." Behind this lies the concealed intention to obtain and collect as much agreement as possible through yes-answers from the financial client. Manipulation occurs with these questions for agreement insofar as an attempt is made to "lull" the conversation partner, to bring them to one's own side, and to give them a supposed or false sense of security.

Another rhetorical trick is the use of the subjunctive, such as "Imagine you *could* invest …€, what would be the first thing that comes to mind?" or "If you *were* retired, how high should your income be to finance your well-deserved retirement?" It may seem as if the financial advisors, for example, have "looked over the shoulder" of car salespeople and copied some sales tricks! When car salespeople start a conversation with the subjunctive with the words *"If you were to buy a new car"* …, they automatically rely on the visual imagination and realization of opportunities or possibilities, as well as the pleasant sensations triggered, which arouse desires and cravings associated with an increase in emotional excitement in their customers. That this leaves "rational thinking" by the wayside is probably obvious and certainly intended!

Consultants or salespeople who use the subjunctive are, colloquially speaking, applying the method "You catch more flies with honey." This is nothing more than making the customer "salivate" with imaginative mental images and awakening dormant needs that push for fulfillment and satisfaction. From a sales strategy perspective, this method serves the purpose of *"turning implicit (needs) into explicit demand"* (see Wienkamp, 2021a, p. 14).

10.3.1.2 Personnel Consulting

Why do HR managers need personnel consulting? Not because the affected executives in the line or HR are incompetent or at a loss, but because they want to leverage the specialized know-how of the consulting industry to achieve even more optimal personnel management or to better secure important personnel strategic decisions. For example, one might think of the search and acquisition of senior executives in and for "key positions" or high-caliber specialists, who can sometimes only be approached through headhunters.

Headhunters pull out all the stops of social influence to, on the one hand, get in contact with the "target persons" at all, and on the other hand, to make a possible job and often perspective change "appealing" to them during the conversation. Their "knowledge capital" consists of insider information about these "candidates for change," such as a certain dissatisfaction with the current "job," perhaps because the current career development has not gone as desired, the "urge for new horizons" to perhaps "reinvent" oneself, and possibly atmospheric disturbances in the current company. Such information can only be obtained through confidential conversations with informants in a "social network," such as former clients or employers.

Headhunting is certainly the most exclusive form of personnel selection. But even for vacancies for "normal" applicants, who were previously acquired through job advertisements and selected and proposed via aptitude diagnostics, personnel consultants are increasingly relying on the social media of professional networks or using their diverse contacts to find suitable candidates.

Consultants can assert their special influence in the determination and specification of requirement profiles. Most of the time, requirement profiles are already fixed after conducting a "psychological requirement analysis" (see Wienkamp, 2020c, 2021a, b, 2022c) and are available as a basis for orientation and decision-making with their concrete characteristics. However, it may also be that personnel consultants want to set new impulses based on, for example, current experiences from their previous mandates, not least to impress their new clients and "stroke" their own ego. Their "impression management" is primarily intended to convey to the client how important they are for him in the personnel search.

Unfortunately, it is also the case that consultants, out of competitive thinking, are not immune to chasing after trends in personnel management and basking in the light of "glamorous," often English-language technical terms that sound particularly nice and highlight and suggest special personnel or management qualities. In the past, the word "teamwork" was certainly on everyone's lips and found in every job advertisement or posting; today, or recently, it is or was most likely "emotional intelligence"!

Indispensable in the formulation of requirement profiles are definitely the so-called "business requirements" (see Wienkamp, 2021a, p. 40, 2022b, c), such as "business sense," innovation capacity, etc. Introducing business requirements as mere "empty phrases" into the debate about personnel challenges and competencies falls short and is self-prohibitive, as they, like the "classic" personality or work requirements in the past, can only be identified and fixed through a selected methodology to meet a necessary standard and quality level of clarity and precision.

Such a step into a careful investigation prevents the whispering of glamorous buzzwords as requirement criteria, which are often and unfortunately not even approximately defined, and many understand different things by them. In the worst case, such "word quibbles" gain influence over clients and HR managers if not countered and questioned and discussed through an objective and always verifiable investigation procedure and then substituted. Dishonest manipulation intentions on the part of personnel consultants, if the temptation existed and there was an initial approach, are curbed, prevented, and made obsolete or superfluous by methodological standards and quality criteria!

Sometimes, however, organizations are also looking for a certain type of person as an "ideal employee," who knows everything, can do everything, and is always successful; the "universally talented employee" (Wienkamp, 2021a), or as Malik (1998) called it: the "universal genius," is then in demand! However, this prototype does not exist in our working world, and due to today's division of labor, it does not need to exist. If a personnel consultant suggests to the company to search for such "exotic birds" or "supermen," it would be pure "window dressing," mixed with unfortunate manipulation attempts that indicate nothing more than self-marketing or even blindness to reality.

Personnel consultants could proceed with educational and training measures in a similar way as with the requirement characteristics with their clients and mean well by them when they promote their latest programs, which, comparable to exceptional management and work requirements, are also adorned with euphonious labels and represent something "like the latest trend" in the education market. Especially the motivation programs for the supposed increase in performance capacity and willingness to perform are a supposedly "good" (thus rather a bad) example of this. Unreflective team-building measures as well as exotic creativity techniques also belong to this genre. Not to mention the esoteric self-awareness courses, which are sometimes touted as special educational offerings for personal development.

In personnel development, personnel consultants are often found conducting coaching measures, on the one hand because of their psychological know-how, their professional experience, and their independence in their work, and on the other hand for reasons of confidentiality, as they are naturally obliged to confidentiality and discretion for all personal information learned from the client for professional ethical reasons. Similar to a supervisor or coach in sports, they work with recommendations that the client examines for themselves, tries out if necessary, and then implements in practice in a manner suitable to them to get closer to their planned personal development goals.

Attempts at influence are almost expected from a consultant during outplacement measures when it comes to motivating the affected employees either for retraining and supporting and emotionally accompanying them in their entry or making them fit for an application process in the job market, and thus for a new professional future, through appropriate behavior training.

Sometimes it can be helpful and useful to, so to speak, "put oneself on stage," including one's own actions or behavior and the methodology and work organization used so far. For example, Eisenführ (2001, pp. 151 ff.) reflected on the appointment process for a professorship in the form of an epilogue and analyzed it according to the standard of "rational decision-making" (see Chap. 8) "after the deed was done" with the aim of learning from mistakes or shortcomings if necessary and drawing the necessary consequences for further appointment processes.

In the selection of chair holders, it is required and prescribed to create a list of appointments with three ranked candidates by the participants of the appointment committee of a university and then submit this list as a staffing proposal to the Ministry of Science. Naturally, the top-ranked candidate has the "right of precedence" and would be invited by the university or the ministry to contract negotiations about salary, funding, and other conditions.

Most of the next-ranked applicants are aware of the outcome of the personnel selection and are only conditionally available as substitute candidates, as they have usually already reoriented themselves or will do so. Should negotiations with the selected candidate fail and none of the substitute candidates are available, the process must be repeated and restarted, with the consequence that one or even two semesters the chair remains vacant. In the professional world, this result of a "vacant chair" and personnel bottleneck is considered a "GAU," that is, the "greatest conceivable accident." To methodically get a grip on this existing uncertainty in some way, it must be operationalized through assumptions of subjective probability expectations, which are based on the personal circumstances of the applicants and the applicant motivation derived from them, and integrated into the calculation model.

Since a university is quite free in the procedure of appointing professors, how it designs the selection process and according to which standards and decision criteria it intends to proceed, the approach to maneuver criticism or analysis and reflection lay in the past process of professor search and selection itself. Thus, it is understandably important for a university, above all, to focus on the quality of research, which is to be demonstrated by the number of publications in renowned publications. Next, the applicant should have good, or at least satisfactory, didactic skills for conducting courses, which are to be evidenced by references and a teaching sample. Finally, management experience and willingness to cooperate in the "research community" can still be desirable criteria in the selection.

In the subsequent review of the selection process, it has now been shown that the absolute number of research publications is still not very meaningful if the professional time and the elapsed time since the last publication are not considered and weighted. In addition, the weighting of the other selection criteria such as didactics, management experience, and willingness to cooperate was to be reexamined and discussed. Furthermore, it turned out that strategic ambitions or goals of the university had not yet been in focus, i.e., the question of what the university aims to achieve with its faculties in the future as a performance profile and what they want to offer their chair holders so that they, on the one hand, go along with it, on the other hand, have the desired potential as scientists. In other words, from the university's perspective, it is about the question: "Who are we actually looking for?"

Without wanting to abandon the methodology according to the "Rational Decision Theory," it seems sensible, based on the experiences made, to review the relevant selection criteria and, if necessary, to reweight them and incorporate them into the "additive value model" (see Sect. 8.2) in a newly modified form and use them.

10.3.1.3 Other Consultations

From the spectrum of further or other consultations, consumer consultations and social consultations as public-law institutions should be mentioned here and particularly appreciated against the background of general or commercial requests for assistance. Social consultations can also be the start of a subsequent therapy (such as a recently offered financial therapy; see Sect. 11.1) if the issue requires it.

If someone is asked about consumer consultation, the respondent is likely to think of nothing spectacular or surprising. Consumer consultations have a public advisory mandate and are intended to protect consumers from unlawful transactions or to address their negative consequences in a socially acceptable manner and in the interest of the consumer, and, if possible, to bring the advisory mandate to a tolerable and fair conclusion.

Consumer questions or problems abound and occur in all areas of our modern consumer world. Whether, for example, excessive electricity or communication tariffs or other questionable business practices are the cause of the problem is one thing. The response to this is then the active support by the advisory centers for or in the interest of those affected in solving their sometimes not easy contractual problems.

If necessary, consumer advisors take on a supervisory mandate (for a manageable fee) to protect or enforce the rights of their clients by, for example, bringing and representing their concerns before arbitration boards if the provider or creditor does not move and shows no willingness to compromise. At the latest then, as in other consultation cases, the advisors face their responsibility and the "public interest" with the tasks derived from it, so that consumers are willing to give up a bit of their maturity and self-responsibility. In other words: They voluntarily place themselves in the hands of the advisor and allow themselves to be influenced by him (or her)—usually manipulated in their own interest and to their own advantage!

Unlike lawyers or other advisors, the advisors in consumer consultation pursue no self-interests that, if you will, concern the "own wallet." In this respect, they have a public function and are charitable.

Social consultations mostly concern questions or matters in shaping one's own life in the facets that have led to problems in coping with typical everyday situations. People with these difficulties can no longer cope with the challenges of certain problems or conflicts and then turn in their helplessness to social consultation, such as family or parenting counseling centers, or in commercial matters or problems, for example, to debt counseling.

After an initial acquaintance or contact conversation, "it comes to the crunch," because the previously non-binding conversation, if the client wishes, turns into a proper and official supervisory mandate. Debt counselors then, for example, conclude a supervisory contract with the debtor, which obliges the debtor to submit to the directives of the advisor in their own interest until the end of the mandate (which is usually also the end of the personal bankruptcy). Otherwise, the care supervision by the debt counseling would come to an end. Only after a regulation successfully obtained or agreed upon by the debt counselor with the creditors, possibly also through a formal personal bankruptcy, would the debtor be autonomous again in their decisions and released from the mandate.

Comparable to a sports coach, a supervisory relationship develops from the mandate of a social consultation, which has to successfully master pedagogical or educational tasks, such as long-term debt counseling/supervision. Whether direct instructions or rather subtle behavioral influence is already what is generally understood as manipulation is debatable. Be that as it may, manipulations or "behavioral controls to one's own advantage" in social consultations with an official mandate are absolutely necessary and normal.

10.3.2 Negotiations

Negotiations serve either the distribution or sale of products and services or they are the subject of disputes aimed at resolving conflicts through amicable agreement or balancing interests. Authors from conflict research then speak of a "win-win situation" as the ideal state.

Negotiations are anything but predictable and boring; rather, they characterize situations full of tension, with unforeseen developments or surprises and their own dynamics—a state that not all people enjoy and not everyone likes. Despite the undeniable moments of surprise, negotiations are not a battle for the rigorous enforcement of one's own interests, but the negotiating partners try to find or forge a compromise, which presupposes an informative dialogue.

Without a reached balance of interests, one would assume a dictate (as a "dictated peace" is called in politics as the submission of the weaker opponent after a military confrontation), where the stronger party virtually dictates the conditions to the weaker side and is at most willing to make small or cosmetic concessions. Another variant would be the ultimatum, where the weaker opponent is offered a negotiation package as a "compromise solution" that he (or she) can only accept or reject (i.e., "take it or leave it"). Unlike in the ultimatum game, the stronger party loses nothing and suffers no disadvantages if the negotiation solution is rejected (see Sect. 6.2.2.2).

Both for sales negotiations and for negotiations for other reasons, there are some rules of play or conduct that must be strictly adhered to and observed if negotiations are to end successfully. Generally, negotiations follow a "7-step communication model" (see, for example, Kunkel et al., 2006) from preparation to the inevitable closing ritual or possibly the follow-up.

An important rule is "not to rush things," that is, to pursue and follow a strategy of "probing," as I would call it. Even with the most intensive preparation, it cannot be ruled out that not all relevant and important information is "on the table" and known. Thus, "hypothetical questions" of the type: "What if…?" can stimulate the imagination and allow new insights into the opponent's initial situation, leading to new findings that positively influence the further negotiation phases and bring the solution a step closer. In this context, it would also be helpful and tactically clever, as in billiards, to "play off the cushion," for example, with the statement "What could be a fair compromise or price?"

Since, as a rule, all negotiations go through a certain sequence or chain of negotiation phases, it is important at the beginning to have an extensive exchange of information to a) get to know each other, b) stimulate thought processes or "thinking," and c) outline a negotiation framework (i.e., "What are we actually talking about?"). With several negotiation points, such as compensation for damages, pain and suffering, etc., it is essential to avoid focusing or narrowing down to one aspect or negotiation point, as this only leads to a dead end. The urge of the psyche for simplification, or to "get some air," via the detour of self-disclosures (such as expressions of displeasure or similar) to the current critical phase, which is causing enormous pressure or stress, should not be given in to. Emotions at the wrong time indicate a lack of emotional distance and offer additional points of attack in a shaky or weak negotiating position. Unfortunately, according to current experience, those who feel threatened in their foundations tend to overreact and risk losing touch with reality, as the psyche now automatically switches to "autopilot" (as a fixed behavior program). Therefore, insinuations, false claims, or even lies, which can occur involuntarily as "displacement activities" under psychological pressure but lead to nothing, should be avoided at all costs. On the contrary, they are later regretted because they have massively damaged or led to the breakdown of the negotiation process.

If, in the heat of the moment, a negotiation gets stuck and ends up in a dead end, it is better, besides taking a break or a negotiation pause, to "downshift" and start again at an earlier negotiation phase, such as the information phase. Apparently, there had been misunderstandings or information gaps that needed to be clarified afterwards.

Successful negotiations, as will be explained in more detail below as sales negotiations and other negotiations with the aim of balancing interests or reaching a compromise, always end, as they have since "time immemorial," with a ritual. This can be a nod of agreement, a handshake, or the signing of a contract.

10.3.2.1 Sales Conclusion

Sales negotiations are a special case of negotiations in general, but certainly the most widespread and popular conception or variant of them!

According to the general understanding of how marketing works, ideally, sales negotiations should not be necessary at all, as the goal is for the sales conclusion to occur without negotiations due to the marketing and sales promotion measures employed. In other words, the consumer is already so inspired or emotionally stimulated by the advertising or product presentation (e.g., through an appealing window display) that he (or she) absolutely wants to satisfy his need by acquiring the desired goods. Need arousal and need fulfillment are thus the "key concepts" or principles of consumer psychology and the marketing mix. A rogue who thinks evil of it, that this is not a hidden and subtle manipulation!

Sales talks take place independently of specific marketing activities in other forms as well, e.g., as "door-to-door sales" or "doorstep sales." In this type of sales activity, which is preferred by structured sales organizations for acquiring magazine subscriptions or other product sales such as insurance, encyclopedias, etc., the initial goal is to gain entry into the home to then arouse purchase interest through an "informal" product presentation. In technical terms, this is called, for example, "turning implicit into explicit need (or benefit)" (Wienkamp, 2021a, p. 14) or developing it, as has been pointed out in another context. Skilled salespeople use cunning secret sales tricks by first sympathizing with the customer's situation and trying to alleviate any fears, such as "being ripped off." Secondly, they elevate him (or her) in his position as, for example, a parent, critical consumer, or simply as an "important person" onto an "imaginary pedestal," so that he (or she) also experiences himself as important at that moment (e.g., through the formulation: *"You in this position or in your role, for example, as a parent...."*).

Flattery is the special "weapon" of "door-to-door salespeople," on which they rely and which apparently is very effective. This is nothing other than pure social influence or manipulation!

If, on the other hand, formal sales negotiations occur, they must first be planned or scheduled. Buyers (or consumers) and sellers then meet at an agreed time at a specific location. The initiative for this can come from either side. If the initiative comes from the seller, he understandably has specific sales intentions in mind. If the customer takes the initiative, he is either looking for a specific product and conducting his individual "market research" by extensively informing himself at various providers or stores before making a decision, or the prospective buyer is not yet ready in the process and just wants to gather information and take a closer look. For example, when searching for a new car or property, the need for information about all product features and prevailing conditions (including price) is paramount. Only with a sufficient market overview does the prospective buyer feel able to make a fundamental decision about the purchase or acquisition based on the available offers.

When it comes to the "moment of truth," that is, the concrete purchase intention, the customer enters into sales negotiations to achieve the "best" negotiation result for him. For the seller(s), this opens up a wide field as a "social arena" to play out their sales repertoire of "compelling" arguments (or the so-called USPs—Unique Selling Propositions) or "dirty tricks," which are nothing other than manipulation maneuvers.

Sales negotiations that proceed regularly are ultimately nothing other than achieving a balance of interests for both parties, as also occurs in other situations without a sales conclusion, e.g., in an out-of-court or court settlement.

10.3.2.2 Balance of Interests

Negotiations that are not purely sales talks strive for a balance of interests or a compromise solution. The best examples from the working world are dismissal protection processes, which mostly end either through an out-of-court or a court settlement with the payment of an agreed severance payment or similar. Collective bargaining between trade unions and employers' associations is another well-known example of a balance of interests, which ends in a collective agreement, before, during, or after a strike.

Negotiation solutions as a balance of interests are fundamentally always the core of civil legal disputes or litigation procedures. As already in the case of "damage regulation" (see Sect. 7.2.1), the positions or claims are usually far apart at the beginning, so that only step by step and through a laborious process a amicable settlement as a conceivable compromise beckons and finally comes about. Another illustrative example is a divorce proceeding with a sometimes difficult-to-achieve balance of interests before the family court.

Both negotiating partners are well advised not to be tempted by overconfidence about their own negotiating position or by too vivid imaginations or wishful thinking during preparation, because "things usually turn out differently than you think!" It is more skillful (and can also be considered a sign of politeness) to ask or encourage the other side to present their view of things first at the opening of the negotiation and to let them finish without interruption. Ideally, the other side states their demands as a price expectation or procedural proposal right at the beginning. If this move does not work because the opposing party appears irritated or feels ambushed and rejects this request, the "upper limit" should be presented when stating one's own claims and used as a stake. In psychology, this is referred to as a reference point or anchoring effect, which serves one's own advantage and to which both sides can orient themselves.

Together with the "best" argument, which ideally should be presented as justification before stating or announcing any demands or claims, the negotiating party creates a very good starting position if it does not allow itself to be irritated and distracted by (weaker) counterarguments and sticks to the "strongest" argument and repeats it over and over again—after all, the other side should "bite their teeth" on it!

Manipulators then face the unfortunate and difficult task of having to take two steps at once: a) They must get the other party to question or abandon their view or negotiating position and b) to join and share the opinion or argumentation of their opponent.

Finally, after a lively exchange of arguments and counterarguments, a compromise or negotiation solution process is likely to emerge, which requires a certain flexibility and "communicative smoothness" (Wienkamp, 2021a, p. 15) from both sides and is also gradually longed for and desired from a psychological perspective.

A psychological advantage is gained by the negotiating party that makes the "last" concession to the other side, as it creates the (supposed) impression on the opponent of having "negotiated well," even if this is not objectively true and is actually a manipulation maneuver to feign a "pseudo-reality." It is essential to avoid "piling on" or "nagging," that is, demanding a last concession oneself, as this only creates anger and resentment and leaves a "bad aftertaste."—In such a negotiation outcome, the revenge or retaliation of the opponent is almost certainly pre-programmed and to be expected. Such negotiations usually end anything but harmoniously and in good agreement!

10.3.3 Interrogations

Criminal investigators are primarily interested in suspects and incriminating witnesses in the context of securing evidence. Their main focus is logically the search for the main suspect to convict him or her as the perpetrator.

Interrogations of suspects and questioning of non-suspect witnesses are not comparable in the planning and design of the conversation or interrogation method in their intensity and dramaturgy.

10.3.3.1 Suspects

In the interrogation of suspects or defendants, either solid evidence (e.g., fingerprints or DNA traces) or at least heavily incriminating indications such as video recordings, witness descriptions, or similar are already available. In the interrogation, the defendant can only refute these indications if he or she manages to present a "watertight" alibi. If a relieving alibi is lacking because the suspect was allegedly alone at home at the time of the crime, either watching TV or sleeping, the process of the burden of proof goes into the next round if the suspect refuses to confess.

At this point at the latest, investigators or interrogation specialists must resort to social influence techniques, which also include and encompass ambivalent subliminal hints or assertions as a means of creating uncertainty.

First of all, they need to do some preliminary work with which they can confront the possible perpetrator. This includes:

"a) possible previous convictions either in the same matter such as robbery or theft or in general (e.g., animal cruelty in youth often precedes the violent crimes of serial offenders),
b) the search for a motive for the crime, which is essential and sometimes decisive in crimes involving physical violence due to, for example, a relationship conflict,
c) a perpetrator profile or psychogram created by a profiler, which is to be compared for similarity and congruence with the personality profile of the accused, and
d) the review and systematization of crime scene traces and witness statements for relevance to this suspect."

10.3 Communication Level

Withthe help of this information and findings, the criminal investigators plan anddesign the interrogation, during which they confront the suspect with their evidencein a targeted and varied manner and pay attention to contradictions in hisstatements, as they could indicate lies and falsehoods. Influence techniques, suchas hypothetical questions, leading questions, and persistent questioning about-details and specifics, such as exact times, use of possible routes or stations nearthe crime scene that the suspect visited, and their chronological order, etc., aretheir tools.

According to experts (e.g., Schauer, 2022, p. 209), interrogation specialists must also consider that previous convictions or similar should not impair objectivity in judgment formation, which can happen if the "prolongation effect," as I would call it, sneaks in as a pronounced prejudice under the motto "Once a thief, always a thief" or "Once a liar, always a liar"! Whether the phenomenon of the "self-fulfilling prophecy" also occurs in interrogations cannot be easily answered, although this peculiar or irrational behavior would be nothing other than a prejudice and could prove to be a gross error or misjudgment!

Even after several rounds of interrogation, the accused may still refuse to confess, so the existing evidence must be critically assessed to determine whether a charge is possible and pre-trial detention is to be ordered by the criminal judge (in the case of substantial and clear evidence, it would usually suffice for a charge) or whether the suspect is (for the time being) released.

If the suspect is indeed a criminal, possibly with several relevant previous convictions, so that the suspicion is not so far-fetched, increasing irritations must be expected during the interrogations, as such characters have no scruples about sending "will-o'-the-wisps" to create confusion on the investigators' side. Such behavior would correspond to their abnormal character as psychopaths and criminals.

Eysenck (e.g., 1977) is known to have developed the construct of psychoticism (see also Sect. 4.1.2.1), which he used for characterizing abnormal behavior. The proximity or similarity to the character type of a psychopath, and thus often a criminal, should not be overlooked and is noticeable based on the existing behavior descriptions. In earlier publications, Eysenck cited some behavior patterns or character images, such as a) an overvaluation of the present (i.e., the "here and now") to achieve quick gratification, b) emotional coldness (i.e., the absence of any empathy), c) lack of guilt feelings (i.e., what is commonly referred to as "conscience"), and d) disrespect towards other people and institutions (such as teachers or educators).

On the psychoticism scale of the "E–N–P" or the "EPQ" test, psychoticism is further characterized by the following descriptions: a) loner behavior, meaning the person knows only themselves and their interests, b) maladjusted social behavior, c) inhuman and cruel, d) insensitive, e) sensation-seeking, f) aggressive and hostile, g) reckless, and h) enjoys fooling others (see Eysenck, 1977, p. 69). Another typology assumes, on the one hand, a sub-type: aggressive-demanding, and on the other hand, a sub-type: passive-parasitic in psychopaths, which was already pointed out earlier. Unlike normal individuals, psychopaths are particularly unpredictable and incalculable, which also explains their tendency to lie without any feelings of guilt.

Thus, it also explains why a lie detector test does not necessarily react with psychopaths or suspected criminals, as they, unlike normal people, do not show neurophysiological reactions when they lie, and then pass the test with a negative result, i.e., without any noticeable finding indicating criminal behavior or the alleged denial thereof (see Eysenck, 1977, p. 147). Psychopaths, as already mentioned (see Sect. 4.1.2.1), like extroverts, are difficult or poorly conditioned, which could explain their emotionally cold behavior that largely comes without fear and guilt feelings. Additionally, they seem to have a lower cortical arousal level, which indicates and explains their constant craving for sensation and stimulation needs (see Eysenck, 1977, pp. 162 f.).

From forensic psychiatry, there are still interesting and possibly explanatory indications of stress, on the one hand, the observation that those who cannot deal with their own psychological suffering or problems and try to suppress or choke them during interrogation, most likely have the need to pass on the suffering they have experienced to other people and to take revenge for it. The same motive is likely present, on the other hand, if the interrogated person gives the impression that they have been excluded from a "beautiful perfect world" and have always come up short in their life, which only increased the malignant drive for malice (see Adshead & Horne, 2022, pp. 76 and 203).

Thus, those responsible for interrogations and interviews have a special responsibility and task to pay particular attention to the subtle tones and hints in the statements and often "read between the lines," which might reveal the hidden motive or inferiority complex in the respondent's answers or reactions, which could also explain the defensive or manipulative behavior.

10.3.3.2 Witnesses

Unlike suspects, witnesses are not under suspicion of a crime. Witnesses are supposed to simply and straightforwardly testify to what they have seen or heard as their observations, regardless of whether they have made descriptions of people or other situational observations (e.g., a specific car type, perhaps even with the license plate number). It rarely happens that an otherwise unsuspected witness becomes so entangled in contradictions that he (or she) develops into a suspect and actually becomes one.

What witnesses experienced or saw has "emotional relevance" (see Arntzen, 2011, p. 9). The witness examination, or a subsequent credibility assessment of the witness statement by a neutral expert, is therefore nothing other than a reconstruction of events or occurrences that took place in the past and to which the witness should remember as well as possible.

Experts or specialists use "intra-individual comparisons" to verify the credibility of witness statements by comparing statements about the course of events with deliberately induced fantasy productions both quantitatively and qualitatively, or, as Arntzen (2011, pp. 11 f.) described it: "Insightful … is the relationship between the experiential performance and the fantasy performance of the respective witness and the comparison of these two (cognitive) performances with the present statement." It is difficult for any subject to invent suitable details in the imagination that also fit together and create something like a "story" or episode, as if an event had been experienced firsthand. Hardly anyone possesses so much "artificial empathy" to immerse themselves so deeply into imaginative and fictional situations as epistemic, i.e., self-experienced perceptions or experience-based knowledge.

If the (alleged) experiences are presented quickly, i.e., at an appropriate speed, it can be assumed that they are valid, i.e., credible, and were remembered and replicated without additional considerations or fantasy performances. A witness statement is perfectly formed when it reproduces a proper experiential story ("their own story") with all necessary and existing details. The repetition rate of *non-experienced* events is about 10% after a few weeks (see Arntzen, 2011, p. 51) and provides an impressive indication that truthful statements have permanence and are well imprinted and established in memory.

In addition to the comments already presented on lies or false statements (see Sects. 2.4, 3.5 and 4.1.2.5), attention should also be drawn to the characteristics in a credibility assessment for detecting false statements:

"1) a disciplined effort to convince (or influence) others during questioning;
2) no disordered or confused presentation of the described; rather, the opposite is the case, as the respondent or witness strives for coherence;
3) the thoughts are organized in the statements, e.g., by mentioning cause and effect or similar."

Accordingto Arntzen (2011, p. 107), implausiblestatements lack the "structure of credibility features" that give the statement itscharacter, such as the level of detail, precision, homogeneity of individual parts orperceptions, their objectivity and consistency or stability. Additionally, as alreadymentioned, it depends on the intra-individual comparison between the thoroughness ofexperienced and remembered observations and the mental images in one's own fantasy world(see Arntzen, 1978, p. 73). Only with aminimal frequency of inconsistencies in the criteria to be examined can or should thecredibility of the statements be assumed.

Unbelievable statements do not necessarily have to be lies or deliberate falsehoods; their low informational value is mostly due to the general, vague, or blurred content, which often does not fit well together. If the witness shows classic somatic signs of nervousness or stress, this can be a sign of general tension or even fear of the interrogation. Such signs, like blushing, sweating, etc., are not specific to lies or falsehoods. An increased level of activation due to stress and tension is generally shown by all subjects during a lie detector test.

However, witnesses can also make themselves suspicious in other ways if they accuse or incriminate other persons as suspects due to contrived, personal motives, or conversely, protect possible suspects through false statements (e.g., if they provide them with a false alibi).

For investigators, special demands are placed on the credibility of the witness statement when this witness is also the victim or the injured party or another injured party (e.g., a family member). Understandably, the victim is also concerned with finding not only *the* perpetrator but any *perpetrator* and possibly seeking revenge through accusations. Differentiating between "fiction and truth" is the constant task and challenge for criminologists (see also Chap. 5).

10.3.3.3 Requirements for Evidence in Interrogations

Regardless of whether it is with suspects or non-suspect witnesses, certain requirements must be set for securing evidence during interrogations, which investigators and later, in criminal proceedings, the jurists must observe. First of all, a distinction must be made between pure facts, such as demographic information: date of birth, place of birth, place of residence, etc., as facts, and on the other hand, an opinion about something. An opinion, such as "I consider the person … to be aggressive and evil," does not necessarily correspond to the facts and is certainly not yet evidence. Therefore, only facts that are proven to be true, such as an accurate description of the perpetrator near the crime scene, are relevant for securing evidence. In this assessment, investigators are concerned with what psychological certainty a validity and reliability check of statements and clues provides.

For the probative value of findings or evidence, the following "grading scheme" with the levels of gradation would be appropriate and is introduced and common in practice (see Schauer, 2022, p. 35 f.):

"1) Beyond all reasonable doubt with a probability of over 90% correct;
2) The preponderance of the evidence suggests that … which, although a weaker gradation, would still be plausible;
3) All other statements or clues that do not meet the aforementioned requirements are (initially) irrelevant and do not yet reach probative value as evidence."

Especially "eyewitnesses" could "wander off" if they fall for "hearsay" about events (without specific naming of a source) or only generalities like "Everyone knows that this is the case" and unconsciously and without firm intention make false or incorrect statements. In the worst case, such false or unclear information can lead to innocent people being accused (these would be the false positives or the "false alarms") or guilty people getting away (these would then be the false negatives), which would be equally fatal.

Unfortunately, the consequential principle also applies to interrogations and witness statements: Reality usually has *two* faces!

10.4 Summary

For practice, the advisory cases observed for various reasons are particularly relevant, which are often the prelude to further directive, i.e., instruction-based measures, such as a guardianship mandate or therapeutic treatment.

In the rather voluntarily conducted consultations, such as financial advice, which is frequently or usually sought by private individuals, ambivalent situations or conflicts due to advantage calculations are nevertheless to be expected due to the commercial interest or business connection, especially with banks, insurance companies, or other sales agencies. Consultations, perhaps with the exception of publicly funded social counseling, are not free of charge, but the consulting effort in terms of time and manpower must be amortized in another form, usually through commission-dependent product sales. Personnel consultations, which were also extensively covered here, are order-dependent services provided on behalf of others. Social counseling, on the other hand, pursues charitable purposes and is usually free of charge due to public interest.

Formal negotiations, such as to conclude a business deal, or interrogations that aim to clarify a case or offense, have nothing in common with consultations. Both the pressure to act and the communication channels or influencing methods to be used differ fundamentally from the rather voluntarily occurring consultation cases.

Therapeutic Applications at the Interface Between Counseling and Treatment

Social influences through manipulative interventions by the therapist are not only legitimate in their execution but also absolutely necessary if they serve the recovery and healing success of the patient. In contrast to covert manipulation maneuvers for commercial purposes, the therapist does not pursue hidden and advantageous or self-serving intentions for himself, but rather has only the well-being of the patient and the success of the treatment in mind with his interventions.

In therapeutic applications or procedures, it is primarily about the communication between client and therapist in order to collaborate at all, but also and especially about clarifying relationship issues that are absolutely necessary for the acceptance and success of the (manipulative) therapeutic interventions. Based on the communication methods and relationship patterns, it can be demonstrated and diagnosed how, against the background of the symptoms to be treated, the manipulative interventions are employed and unfold their effect.

Already in the previous Chap. 10 some applications of consulting activities, such as financial consulting, personnel consulting, and in a broader sense social consulting, have been mentioned. In the borderline area of a consulting service, it should have become clear that the transition from consulting, in the sense of giving recommendations, to a supervisory mandate, or also in the financial sector or personnel management as a coaching measure, is fluid, even if due to special circumstances, e.g., because of the necessary know-how, the actors "change the stage." In particular, the transition from pure consulting, e.g., in financial matters, to psychotherapy due to a massive personality problem, e.g., because of gambling or speculation addiction or compulsive consumption, is more or less fluid. Conversely, it is also conceivable that a therapist, in treating psychological problems, also becomes aware of commercial problems or other difficulties.

Using the example of financial therapy, which distinguishes itself as a relatively new form of therapy from the already discussed financial consulting, it will be demonstrated how therapeutic concepts connect with practical questions of daily life management and lifestyle and build on and develop from preceding consulting activities. Conversely, psychotherapists sometimes find in the treatment of psychological disorders or personality problems that the financial behavior of their patient (or the patient) is not sustainable and, if nothing decisive happens, completely "gets out of control," so that due to their lack of competence in specific financial matters, they rely on the support and advice of financial experts or financial coaches (or also lawyers).

11.1 General Information on Financial Therapy

Sometimes, a consultation or similar is not enough, but the existing problem, especially when severe personality disorders cause the manifest problems and either still obscure or exacerbate them, requires professional therapy or treatment by a specialist trained for this purpose. Occasionally, however, it may appear that, for example, a debt counselor in a social counseling service is not only responsible for advising the problem carriers but also enters a phase of support and intervention (e.g., at the beginning or during an ongoing private insolvency), which already exhibits "therapeutic traits" in its approaches to bring about a behavioral modification and solution to the financial problems.

The first point of contact for a client can therefore be, for example, a social counseling center or a financial advisor in special cases, where it is then determined that, for example, behind extreme debt problems lie personality-specific problems or difficulties (here in dealing with money or finances) that cannot be solved with the existing know-how of the advisors. In the absence of accreditation (e.g., licensing) or authorization for this further treatment, its execution by specialists not trained for this, such as psychotherapists, is also prohibited or strictly forbidden for formal and legal reasons. Traditionally, a counselor would then refer the client to, for example, a psychotherapist, who is indeed an expert in mental illnesses, such as compulsive actions, diffuse fears, or depression, but generally is less familiar with the manifest symptoms and their handling in all facets of "financial behavior," such as a debt problem due to purchasing or consumption compulsions or the like. Depending on the severity of the mental illness or personality disorder, psychotherapy may be indicated, which may even be paid for by health insurance (or alternatively against a private invoice).

Representing the entire spectrum of psychotherapeutic procedures and applications, in this context of counseling activities, reference is made to the recently conceived and introduced "financial therapies," which address precisely this interface between financial counseling and the treatment of the causative personality disorders, which then reveal themselves in the everyday life of financial consumers and lead to significant problems in normal life, and offer cooperative pragmatic solutions (see the anthology by Klontz et al., 2015a).

Currently, the only recognized mental illnesses include gambling addiction and the collecting and hoarding of objects and items known as "hoarding disorders," which, as a consequence of too many acquired and collected things, lead to disorder or chaos in the home, making normal living impossible.

Regardless of all therapeutic approaches and concepts, it should be considered that therapists must use manipulative methods in both their diagnostic efforts and the subsequent interventions to, so to speak, bring the client back "on the right track" or "on the path of virtue," i.e., to their "financial recovery" and symptom-free behavior.

Financial therapies have existed as a form of therapy since 2009 in the USA with the founding of the "Financial Therapy Association" (see Britt et al., 2015a, p. 3). It is intended for "financial and mental health practitioners" who operate in the environment of financial counseling, financial coaching, and psychotherapy. The previous research activities ranged from the first systematically conducted studies at universities dealing with this subject or problem with selected clients and students, through "case studies," to still theoretical considerations that have so far been in the experimental stage in practice. For individual issues, such as personality problems and maladaptive behavior patterns in dealing with money and finances, there are both diagnostic tools, such as standardized questionnaires with corresponding scales, and therapy programs with specially created manuals, quasi as "scripts or directions," which emphasize and cover both intrapsychic and interpersonal problems in application.

In contrast to financial counseling, the problems of financial consumers lie either in hidden difficulties in the person or personality development or, in view of certain situational challenges (e.g., in divorce), in the inability to manage financial problems. In other words: Either "money disorders" as personality disorders or a lack of know-how in connection with the necessary self-confidence for "money management" are present!

Both problem areas can be treated through financial therapy, where it is about unresolved emotional conflicts, dysfunctional attitudes (e.g., "life scripts"), and maladaptive behavior, for which the previously known psychotherapeutic concepts are offered. Financial therapies, which may begin with financial counseling or visiting a debt counseling center (see above), can transition into or end in psychotherapy if the personality problem (e.g., gambling addiction or consumption compulsion) demands it.

According to the current state, the psychotherapeutic concept, as in many other treatment areas, is a "technical eclecticism" (see Britt et al., 2015b, p. 19 f.), that is, a "colorful bouquet" of proven and practical applications and methods from different therapy schools—as there is no general or universally accepted psychotherapy in that sense. Some, or most, psychotherapists also describe their approach as an "integrative approach" or "integrative therapy."

11.2 Personality Disorders and Maladaptive Behaviors

Similar to the "life scripts" from transactional analysis (e.g., Berne, 2006), "money scripts" (see Lawson et al., 2015, pp. 23 ff.) are conveyed through upbringing in childhood and adolescence, partly from generation to generation, and shape further life, here the life with financial problems and challenges. These include:

- "Avoidance behavior regarding money ("Money Avoidance") as a negation of financial problems and matters, or the profound aversion to dealing with them at all, due to, for example, irrational attitudes such as "money is dirty and a thing of the devil" or "money is a taboo for me";
- "Money Worship" as the veneration or worship of money or material possessions followed by the attitude "the more money, the better and the happier the person," or the easier it is to gain affection (or love) from others or to "buy" it;
- Excessive money status ("Money Status"), when self-esteem depends "on the size of the bank account" or the wealth status; this also involves the "display" of a desired social status defined by money possession or by an exclusive lifestyle, wanting and being able to afford certain things—in contrast to others;
- Fixation on money ("Money Vigilance") is the constant preoccupation with money and financial issues either due to excessive private "day trading" as a sign or symptom of an emerging addiction to speculation or driven by great distrust of others regarding monetary matters; in this specific context, "quirky" or bizarre behaviors may also appear, such as the general rejection of using credit cards as a common means of payment."

From the presented "money scripts," but not only from them, massive malignant behavioral habits ("Money Disorders") can arise, which manifest in financial life as immense stress due to underlying personality deficits and fears. In particular, the following peculiarities should be considered:

"1) Compulsive buying disorder
   - Purchases triggered by impulses and/or compulsions are made for the purpose of emotional relief and the suppression or elimination of negative feelings;
   - The purchase itself provides satisfaction, not the purpose or the bargain as a "deal";
2) Gambling disorder
   - For the gambler or speculator, it is impossible to stop playing on their own due to the compulsive neurosis;
   - The pursuit of monetary gain through gambling serves self-esteem;
   - Gambling losses do not deter but stimulate the continuation of gambling, to "chase" the supposed win and to want to prove it again and again, which is nothing other than the pathological compulsion to repeat a neurosis;
3) Money hoarding
   - An exaggerated sense of possession (or the "Scrooge McDuck syndrome" from the Walt Disney comic) leads those affected to be unable to part with money and possessions;

- Their identity depends on their possessions, and they define themselves by the acquired objects;
- Fear of loss and distrust drive these people;
4) Financial enabling as a benefactor
    - Behind this is the inability to say "no" to requests for lending money or loans;
    - Money functions as a substitute for "love."

In addition to these critical or malignant personality traits, there are other objectionable behaviors related to financial resources (see Canale et al., 2015, pp. 35 ff.). Among these "money disorders," the tendency towards secrecy or "hide-and-seek" with financial conditions or financial matters, such as covert, secret expenses for personal consumption, should be mentioned, which become noticeable especially towards important reference persons like spouses or similar as a sign of "infidelity" through concealed expenses or the accumulation of secret funds (these are the "financial infidelity"). This personality trait also includes the tendency to declare money or income a taboo topic and to suppress it meticulously and not talk about it. Without restrictions, these "veiled" or concealed actions must be clarified and addressed in therapy. In particular, it is important to uncover their manipulation potential, as it is nothing other than an attempt or action to deceive!

To track down these maladjusted behavioral habits regarding money and finances, previous research has developed a series of diagnostic instruments that can be used as questionnaires (see Sages et al., 2015, p. 69 ff.). These include both income and asset statements or inventories as well as evidence of income and expenses, such as a classic "household book." Ratios derived from a comparison of the asset status, e.g., assets compared to liabilities or debts, or the average liquidity or savings rate as, for example, a monthly surplus (defined as the difference between income minus expenses), complete the financial diagnostics. It should not go unmentioned in this context that there are already very detailed and sophisticated financial control and analysis instruments that are also suitable for these purposes (e.g., the "Financial Navigator" by Wienkamp, 2019).

The questionnaires constructed by Klontz (and others) based on factor analyses and test-theoretical examinations, such as the reliability determination ("Cronbach's Alpha") and the sensitivity of the instruments through group comparisons, deal entirely with the already mentioned "Money Scripts" and "Money Disorders" in detail and attempt to diagnose them using the items developed for this purpose.

11.3 Therapy Forms

Apparently, the "first steps" in the field of financial therapies suggest making the most comprehensive use of the existing psychotherapeutic schools and therapy forms. Depending on the previous practical testing and, if applicable, scientific accompaniment through studies, ideally with a therapy or treatment group and as a comparison a control group, the existing findings on the individual therapy approaches are, to put it mildly, "very manageable." According to the authors Klontz et al. (2015b, p. 117), "Experiential Financial Therapy" is one of the few therapies whose application and healing successes are supported by relevant studies. The following overview may shed some light on the "therapy landscape" in financial therapy (see Table 11.1), whereby this overview only lists the therapy forms or programs identified in the anthology by Klontz et al. (2015a) that were scientifically examined and accompanied according to their own statements.

With the exception of behavioral therapy treatment methods, the listed therapies are rather non-directive, i.e., they are more focused on cooperation and "commitment" between the patient (or client) and the therapist and primarily work with interpretations or reconstructions of past traumatic experiences or give the client the opportunity to face these past experiences once again in the presence of the therapist, in order to relive or cope with them in the here and now. Of course, the "classic" methods from various therapy forms, such as role-playing within the framework of "psychodrama" or the questioning techniques known from systemic therapies (e.g., the "miracle question"), are used here. The main concern of the treating therapist or psychotherapy is to open up new worlds of experience for the patient or client or to provide them with new interpretations of the traumatic events or emotional conflicts, for example, through "reframing," in order to work on their "core conflicts" and gradually distance themselves from or resolve them.

Various therapeutic approaches from practice, such as systemic therapy or psychodynamically oriented procedures, with probably little or no scientific foundation and review for severe personality problems in financial matters, can also be found in the cited publication.

11.4 Case Example as "Case Study"

To better imagine a treatment situation within the framework of financial therapy, a life story with corresponding symptoms will be presented and treated as a fictional case. The biographical details and the described symptoms are entirely fictional, but they could have occurred in real life.

Particular attention in this case description should be paid to the interventions or interpretations of the psychotherapist, which are intended to steer or manipulate the patient or client in a certain direction—naturally for his or her well-being.

11.4.1 Biographical Details

A single woman, let's call her Sabine, aged 39, working as a pharmaceutical sales representative, predominantly visits a fixed clientele of private practice doctors from various specialties. Her net or household income is around €3300 per month, plus travel reimbursements and expenses. Her professional activity requires a

11.4 Case Example as "Case Study"

Table 11.1 Diverse therapy forms for the treatment of psychological problems related to money or financial issues. (Based on Klontz et al., 2015a)

No.	Therapy Form	Short Description	Predominant Symptomatology	Typical Interventions	Current Status and Outlook
1	Experiential Financial Therapy (EFT)	Experiential Therapies (ET) combine a variety of different therapeutic approaches The EFT is based on ET, supplemented by concepts of financial counseling to treat so-called "Money Disorders"	Emotional traumatic experiences such as "Unfinished Business" and beliefs formed in childhood ("Money Scripts") prevent a normal handling of money and finances	Psychodrama and role-playing enable the processing of traumas Through reconstruction ("re-experienced") and "reframing," they gain new meanings and perspectives	Initial studies with fixed therapy programs are available
2	Solution-Focused Financial Therapy	This form of therapy explicitly and consciously does not focus on the problem, but on possible solutions Therefore, it is also called "solution-oriented"	All types of weaknesses, behavioral deficits, and lack of knowledge regarding the handling of money Frustrations and burdens in daily life increasingly become an existential problem, e.g., due to excessive consumer spending and lack of or insufficient debt repayment	Miracle question: ("If the problem were gone tomorrow, what would be different?") Scalings from e.g., 1 to 10 for the status quo, level of suffering, etc. Homework (e.g., review and analysis of the last credit card statement)	Initial studies with fixed therapy programs are available, but not yet published
3	Behavioral Therapy (BT)	Cognitive BT, which primarily addresses malignant attitudes that negatively affect behavior	Incorrect, often unjustified attitudes (e.g., rigid information filters, "all-or-nothing thinking") usually lead to avoidance behavior and the anticipation of negative imagined consequences	Clarification of the situation using the "ABC model" Practicing alternative positive behaviors, e.g., through homework	Various studies in the field of financial planning for different issues are available

(continued)

Table 11.1 (continued)

No.	Therapy Form	Short Description	Predominant Symptomatology	Typical Interventions	Current Status and Outlook
4	Cooperative Therapies	As a supplement for couple or family therapies with the involvement of at least 2 experts (e.g., psychotherapist, financial advisor, or lawyer)	Relationship problems and additional issues in financial matters that complicate living together	Parallel or successive processing of both relationship problems and financial issues based on various therapeutic approaches	Previously tested in real cases at universities by students from various faculties under the supervision of an expert, as well as publication of case studies
5	Mixed Therapies	Mixed therapies from BT and Narrative Therapy	Problems with financial matters in the past are listed in chronological order and processed in the form of stories as a narrative therapy approach	Reconstruction of stressful experiences with the aim of overcoming them through empowerment (but also "unleashing")	A treatment concept, the "Ford Financial Empowerment Model," is available
6	Problem- or Symptom-oriented Therapies	Eclectic integration of various therapeutic approaches for a specific symptomatology	Symptomatology was compulsive buying or consumption, which led to massive debt	Behavior modification through BT approaches and imparting skills in the financial area	Fixed program ("Overshopping Model") based on a pilot study including a control group

well-groomed appearance and a fashionable, but not necessarily conspicuous or extravagant wardrobe.

Sabine lives in a small two-room rented apartment and has been in a steady relationship for about three years. Her partner is not yet willing to move in with her and live together in a shared apartment.

This reluctance is mainly related to Sabine's problem, who has succumbed to a constant compulsion to buy shoes. She no longer knows how many pairs of shoes she owns, but it is likely around 500 pairs! The sheer space required for this quantity of shoes is not only enormous but also, due to the resulting lack of space, disorder, or even chaos, shocking and offensive to her partner. It is further complicated by the fact that Sabine is downright obsessed with the so-called "possession compulsion" and finds it incredibly difficult to part with even a single pair of shoes, including old or worn-out ones. No wonder there are repeated arguments and conflicts within their partnership or relationship.

Sabine grew up in a normal family with a father and mother and two sisters and lived at home until her university studies in economics. Sabine is the middle daughter by age, her older sister is one year older, and her younger sister is four years younger.

Her older sister and Sabine coincidentally have the same shoe size, 39, so their mother came up with the idea of always buying new shoes for the older sister first, which Sabine would later wear as well. The background of this habit was that the mother liked to see the shoes worn out or simply "used up" so she could dispose of them with a clear conscience before buying new ones. The younger sister was not only unsuitable for this "ritual" due to her age, but she also had a different shoe size, so the shoes of her older sisters would not have fit her anyway.

Sabine felt like a "second-class child" back then and has suffered from this practice of her mother throughout her life. Talking to her parents about this unequal treatment only helped in exceptional cases, but not really. When Sabine was then disappointed and angry, she compensated by eating sweets, which did not necessarily benefit her figure at the time.

Even as a student, Sabine liked to treat herself to a few new shoes and preferred to forgo other things. From her first salary as a marketing assistant in the pharmaceutical industry, she first bought herself a very fashionable but expensive pair of shoes in a noble shoe boutique that only carried Italian brand products, which was not surprising.

11.4.2 Reason for Treatment and Problem Behavior

The passion for buying shoes has, as expected, not subsided but has increased and intensified over the years, which is only too well demonstrated by the large stock of shoes. For Sabine, acquiring or purchasing shoes has led to a *substitute satisfaction*, which she particularly pursues after customer visits. Either she has made a good sales deal with a visited doctor, for which she feels she must reward herself, or after a less successful business, she needs to compensate for her frustration, both of which end in the purchase of new shoes. Occasionally, when she is at home and has nothing better to do, she scours the internet for new fashionable shoes and orders them. If the shoes do not fit or are uncomfortable, she can easily return them (as unworn shoes) within the return period with a return slip.

Since her boyfriend is also very busy with work and frequently on business trips, Sabine is often alone in her apartment. Her leisure activities, concerning hobbies, sports, or culture, are very limited, which is largely due to the financial need for shoe purchases. Besides her colleagues, she does not have a very large circle of acquaintances who could distract her. She still has regular contact with her family, especially her parents. Her two sisters have now started their own families with children and are going their own way. However, the topic of shoes has become a taboo subject in this family, and neither Sabine's current shoe purchases nor the past in the family are discussed.

In earlier times, Sabine compensated for loneliness and boredom with unrestrained eating behavior, especially with sweets, which occasionally still manifests today in the form of real eating attacks. The excess pounds then necessarily have to be reduced and starved off through diets. Sabine can thus maintain her figure approximately at a normal level today.

From her parents, she learned in her childhood and youth that material possessions are very important and that the purpose of existence and self-esteem are defined by money and possessions, true to the motto "If you have something, you are something!" Her parents also valued making the best possible use of all purchased goods or products to save money in this way as well. Food, for example, never reached its expiration date and never ended up in the trash! From another perspective, experts believe that this "stinginess" or "compulsion to utilize" may have developed into a "family neurosis" at that time.

As already indicated, Sabine not only suffered from this absolute and exaggerated compulsion to utilize, but this compulsion initiated by her family at least contributed to an inferiority complex due to the impression of belonging only to the "second tier," which unfortunately still makes itself felt today in the form of shoe purchases as a compensatory action and balance, with all the negative consequences.

In principle, Sabine has no particular affinity for money and wealth, but her compulsion to buy new shoes has now led to tension and strain on her financial situation.

But at the latest, after her bank account and her credit lines with credit card companies slipped significantly into the "red," i.e., moved to the permissible limit, and her customer advisor at her home bank contacted her and subsequently asked her for a clarifying conversation, Sabine, not least due to her business education and knowledge, grasped and understood the seriousness of her financial situation.

Since she is in a permanent and unresigned employment relationship with a good normal income, the customer advisor advised her to seek qualified counseling and possibly treatment to get her excessive compulsion to consume new shoes under control. Once that is achieved, the financial problems, particularly the account overdrafts, would likely resolve themselves over time.

Sabine then first turned to a debt counseling center. The debt counselor then referred her to a psychotherapist he knew, who is qualified in the area of psychologically induced compulsive actions or compulsive neuroses, due to her particular problem and the not yet impending personal bankruptcy.

11.4.3 Therapy

The psychotherapist is not a designated financial therapist (which, by the way, may not even exist with the corresponding qualification profile), but through the treatment of compulsive neuroses and anxieties, he has often encountered and treated patients with compulsive consumption and the resulting financial problems. He calls his treatment concept "integrative therapy," which is nothing more than a mixture of concepts and intervention techniques from different therapeutic schools, suitable for the symptomatology of compulsive actions and the self-esteem issues often associated with them as a personality disorder.

11.4 Case Example as "Case Study"

Specifically, the therapist is both a proponent of cognitive behavioral therapy (CBT) and a practitioner of psychodynamic as well as humanistic therapy approaches, such as client-centered therapy (CCT) according to Carl Rogers. With CBT, both the malignant attitude complexes and the development of alternative purposeful behaviors are to be worked on. Psychodynamic therapy concepts are primarily intended to discover and work through the life history and any long-standing traumas (i.e., "original conflicts") and to help the patient achieve a better sense of life and self-worth. Humanistic treatment methods primarily serve appropriate communication and a "culture of understanding" and are a prerequisite for building a sustainable therapist-patient relationship.

The treatment goal for Sabine is not only the reduction of shoe purchases as a substitute satisfaction but also the development of new behaviors that serve both daily life management (such as adjusting consumer spending to financial circumstances) and future life planning (including leisure activities, interests, and relationships or acquaintances). Therefore, it is required of the therapist to make the prospect of a "better life" appealing to the patient and to set (manipulative) incentives to support and encourage her. Additionally, work must be done on false or negative attitudes and childhood memories to ensure a better or more positive self-image in connection with more self-confidence and vigor (or empowerment).

To understand Sabine's issues at all and to gain her trust, the therapist initially endeavored to build a resilient relationship by showing her much acceptance and "compassionate understanding" (empathy). It was helpful for him to encourage Sabine to describe her emotional experiences both in the present when buying new shoes and in remembered, past events, and to reflect these descriptions back to her through empathetic acknowledgment as feedback. Similar to the approach in solution-oriented therapies, the therapist not only focused on problems and difficulties but also tried to discover positive aspects, such as "the exception to the rule," and to make Sabine aware of these, giving her hope and confidence. With the confirmation received from the client on the feedback he provided, the therapist also gained important and relevant diagnostic insights.

In a similar manner, he also dealt with her childhood experiences with shoes and tried to make Sabine understand that what happened back then cannot be undone or reversed. The psychotherapist interpreted the preference for her older sister when it came to new shoes not as conscious unequal treatment or even "withdrawal of love" by her parents or her mother, but as the inevitable consequence of the prevailing "family complex" of having to and wanting to utilize and consume everything, in order to act and live economically, we can also say, in an economically rational or "optimizing" manner. With this so-called "reframing" as an intervention from the "toolbox" of relevant psychotherapies (see Table 11.1), the prerequisite for detachment from this traumatic experience and thus for emotional relief should be created. Today, it is primarily about emotionally accepting this as the past, thereby reducing or weakening the urge for substitute satisfaction and compensatory actions.

From the arsenal of methods in CBT, the therapist primarily relies on the assignment and completion of homework between each two therapy sessions.

After the first session, he agreed with Sabine that in the meantime, she should look at her financial documents and check what should be prioritized next (or first) (e.g., reducing the overdraft with the highest interest rate). Additionally, Sabine should, if it occurs, record all purchases of new shoes during this time and sum them up as expenses, without the requirement to particularly restrict herself. This consumption expenditure for shoes during this period should then serve as a "baseline" for comparisons with consumer spending, especially for shoe purchases, in later treatment phases. The purpose of the "before-and-after consideration" (as a retrospective) is to reinforce behavior and thus an influencing measure through this reward process (see also Table 11.1).

For later treatment appointments, the homework was, for example, to create a list of all income and expenses for a month to determine the monthly liquidity requirement. Then Sabine was instructed, when she is about to buy shoes again, to consider beforehand and write down what type of shoes, e.g., winter boots, sandals, sports shoes, etc., she intends to buy, and to strictly adhere to this list; under no circumstances should she make multiple purchases of the same type, possibly in different shoe stores, nor buy any other shoes that were not on the list. If Sabine does not buy all the planned shoes or no shoes on that day, that would also be fine. The motto was no additional shoe purchases *outside* this list!

According to statements from the professional literature (see e.g., Klontz et al., 2015c, p. 349), resistance or unwillingness from patients is to be expected in approximately 80% of therapeutic interventions or treatment recommendations. Apart from the fact that the patient has not yet reached the point in the ongoing therapy that the therapist has already anticipated and desired, and this disturbance is more of a process or communication problem that needs further clarification and resolution, psychological resistance due to fears and defensive attitudes must also be expected in treatment suggestions or inquiries.

If the therapist, for example, suggests to Sabine to classify her collection of shoes into A) new shoes and "favorite shoes," B) other everyday shoes that are still in use, and C) old shoes that have not been worn for a long time, she might protest or have some objections, as she generally has the problem of parting with her shoes as possessions. The background of this requirement or recommendation would be to dispose of some of the old shoes to create space in the apartment. It is to be suspected and cannot be ruled out that this suggestion will probably meet with little approval and will be emotionally rejected by Sabine, if not even vigorously opposed. In the case of strong resistance, the therapist could, for example, counter and ask if she has another suggestion for gaining space or creating order, or suggest starting with just one room and sorting and possibly disposing of the shoes only in that room. The counter-proposal of possibly renting a larger apartment with more space would also be possible and might prompt the patient to think and reflect. This contrast between either creating order in the old apartment or moving to a larger apartment with higher expenses such as rent and moving costs also serves to influence or control behavior.

Sometimes it makes sense to directly address the underlying emotions such as fears or stress to show that the defensive attitude against practical solutions is only related to these conflict-laden emotions, and the underlying hidden conflict inevitably becomes noticeable and must first be addressed. Offers to see past conflicts and current behavioral resistances in a different light or from another perspective, thus giving them a different meaning in the course of "reframing," can help and provide relief and reduce or eliminate fears and resistances, as already demonstrated in the example of unequal treatment in childhood by parents.

Perhaps the therapist should also address Sabine's eating behavior. Sabine seems to be able to compensate for occasional eating escapades with a disciplined diet. As in solution-oriented therapy, this therapeutic context should also be approached in a strength- or resource-based manner, as it is a strong commendable achievement by Sabine in how she deals with this problem. It may be appropriate to transfer behavior moments or thought processes focused on renunciation during a diet to the compulsion to consume! Successful behavior patterns of self-discipline in one area of life would simultaneously be "transmission belts" and positive reinforcers for another area with behavioral problems.

After several months of therapy, Sabine should not only have her pathological shoe shopping under control and her finances back on a sustainable basis, but above all, she should think about the future and engage with desirable future plans. This results not only in vitality and self-motivation but also makes life appear in a completely different, more beautiful, and better light. Thus, it would be a worthwhile goal to possibly intensify the relationship with her current partner and consider moving into a shared apartment and to approach and implement this in practice. Should there be any "snags" or cooperation problems in the treatment process, looking back at the path traveled so far in the therapy process always helps as a reinforcement and self-influence mechanism.

"Follow-up appointments" with the psychotherapist at increasingly larger intervals can help avoid or address relapses into the old compulsive problem and, if necessary, treat them anew. If necessary or needed, contact with other specialists or institutions would also be helpful and indicated for the therapist; of course, only with the patient's consent.

11.5 Summary

Psychotherapies, regardless of their theoretical or methodological background, sometimes follow previous counseling cases when the symptoms require it. Using the example of the not too long-known and practiced financial therapy, it should be shown what an integrative or eclectic approach could look like.

For therapeutic practice, it may become increasingly important, as has become clear with psychologically induced problems with a financial background, to seek collaboration with different experts and specialists. This is necessary not least to act in the interest and for the benefit of the client. The case of pathological buying or consumption compulsion exemplarily presented here should have illustrated both the necessity of treatment and the overarching work with methods and techniques from the "therapy world" as well as the collaboration between various experts or specialists of different professions.

In all efforts for new therapeutic approaches and concepts, diagnostic concerns should not be neglected, especially when manipulative impulses and forces came into play both as self-suggestion (e.g., an inner urge or compulsion) and through external influences or manipulations, such as traumatic experiences in the past. But even during treatment, manipulative interventions by the psychotherapist for the patient's benefit are indispensable, especially when there is resistance to proposed therapeutic measures or the treatment process, for whatever reason, stalls.

Educational Concepts for Promoting Learning, Education, and Personality Development

Without a conclusive discussion about educational or pedagogical concerns, the topic "Diagnostics of Manipulations" finds no conclusion. Similar to therapy or medical treatment, educators, teachers, or other personnel responsible, e.g., in corporate training, also assume a supervisory mandate and are responsible for both the learning and behavioral progress as well as the well-being of the individuals entrusted to them (e.g., pupils or students).

Since the 1960s (of the previous century), scientific research, primarily in the USA, has dedicated itself to this topic in the form of multi-year project studies in schools with the aim of promoting and supporting students from underprivileged social classes in their personality development at school (see deCharms, 1979). The metaphor about the relationship or connection between the "master and his or her puppets (in school and teaching)" became particularly popular, which essentially expresses everything about manipulative behavior.

No wonder, because manipulations are the tools of learning psychology, especially in the form of "instrumental learning" or "operant conditioning" with rewards and punishments as reinforcers, as initially investigated in animal experiments. The aim of these studies was to gain insights into the conditions of learning itself and the possibility of bringing about behavior modifications through either approach behavior as desired behavior or avoidance behavior (as negative reinforcement) to refrain from undesired behavior.

Applied to the situation in schools at that time, this meant from the perspective of the researchers involved in this project that it is not so much about the transmission of knowledge by teachers or educators, but rather about intensifying and promoting "emotional learning," as I would call it, and educating schoolchildren or students to become self-responsible and not externally controlled personalities, providing them with all necessary assistance in this developmental process. This pedagogical approach concerns both the developmental goals and content, as well as the methodology to achieve the set goals. Specifically, the developmental goal of *"causal autonomy,"* as deCharms formulated it at the time, was at the forefront, to which teachers can make a significant contribution through their pedagogical skill and positive social influence.

In addition to the intervention-like lesson design by the responsible educator, which contains a considerable degree of influence potential for the benefit of the students, the pedagogical diagnostics of school participants is also characterized by manipulation maneuvers. In the diagnostics of school performance and the behavior associated with the student's personality, both ongoing assessments and classwork, as well as intelligence and performance tests, are used, along with personality tests, which are usually employed through "fantasy tests" as projective methods with the creation of experience-relevant short stories on selected topics, such as self-responsibility, respect for teachers and classmates, etc. Through the subsequent (and manipulative) feedback and discussion, the affected students are encouraged to think or reflect and to modify their behavior.

12.1 Goals and Topics of School Pedagogy and Promotion

Learning psychology already assumed, based on its experimental findings, that learning is acquired either through "Classical Conditioning (CC)," that is, through "signal learning," or, as already indicated, through "Operant Conditioning (IC)" with the implemented reinforcement mechanisms. In CC, an initially neutral stimulus (e.g., a light), which is the CS (or conditioned stimulus), gradually acquires the function of the UCS (or unconditioned stimulus) in connection or in joint occurrence with a physiologically sensitive stimulus (e.g., electric shock or food) during the reaction formation of the test animal or test person. The learning process of the individual consists of the transformation of the UCS property onto the CS. During IC, the desired behavior of the subject is either continuously rewarded, thus reinforced (or manipulated), or prevented by the threat of punishment, thus generating avoidance behavior through the so-called "negative reinforcement."

Since the exhibited behavioral reactions are always accompanied by either positive feelings such as joy, satisfaction, etc., or by negative affects such as pain, emotions or feelings shape the learning behavior, so it is rightly referred to as "emotional learning." With frequent or constant repetition, this process or procedure accompanied by affects is internalized (and stored in the so-called "emotional memory"), so that the behavior henceforth occurs from within itself in similar or comparable situations. With internalization, the prerequisites for "causal autonomy" (deCharms, 1979, p. 19) as a primary developmental goal of education in general and here in school pedagogy have been created, because a person experiences the origin of their actions within themselves and not outside their own person. In the context of these actions, self-suggestion takes place instead of external suggestion.

The performance motivation critically depends on the causal autonomy just mentioned. The focal point in school and teaching is performance motivation,

12.1 Goals and Topics of School Pedagogy and Promotion

which is a component of the motivation concept, such as that of McClelland (e.g., 1987). In addition to performance motivation, power ambitions and attachment motivation are further components of this motivation model. Performance motivation is originally characterized by competition orientation and hard concentrated work, although competitive behavior does not readily and entirely apply to the school environment and—in contrast to the "free economy"—would be completely inappropriate in excessive form in this "social world." On the other hand, the aspect of power is indeed relevant, as students also maintain social interactions with their peers and handle their favor (or power) carefully and not always thoughtfully, so that they can behave both positively (e.g., helpful, attentive, empathetic) and negatively or dismissively (e.g., quarrelsome, selfish, distancing). On the one hand, they keep a close eye on the situation in which they want and need to assert themselves, and on the other hand, the advantages and disadvantages for themselves that could result as consequences of their behavior (cf. deCharms, 1979, p. 57). However the students behave, their behavior is always embedded in social interactions and shaped by social influence attempts.

Strictly linked to performance motivation is a realistic assessment of one's current abilities. Schoolchildren who have unrealistic or no ideas about their performance capacity either set themselves too low or overly ambitious goals that are completely unrealistic and illusory, ultimately relying on their luck. One motive for this misjudgment is that it is embarrassing for them in front of others if they reveal their performance limits or if it becomes clear that they do not even know them themselves. They prefer to obscure their inability to realistically assess performance and try to conceal it with all their might (cf. deCharms, 1979, p. 78). It should also be clear that unrealistic ideas do not positively influence and promote self-responsibility as another developmental goal! In these attempts at concealment lies also the attempt of defense and deception as manipulative behavior.

Attachment motivation can be closely related to the development of ego ideals as personal developmental goals in the upbringing of children and adolescents, which are acquired and promoted through identification with a significant reference person for the student (e.g., the teacher) through model learning. Most of the time, the affected students take this reference person as a role model.

In the "Master-Puppet Model" propagated by deCharms (1979), it is also interesting that pupils usually go through different developmental stages in their "school career," in which they can alternately be both puppet and master. Depending on the personality type, they develop further in these developmental phases both from the original puppet to the master and along the qualitatively different stages. The following developmental stages are assumed (see deCharms, 1979, p. 172):

- "the impulsive phase;
- the defensive phase;
- the conformist phase;
- and the mature phase (as a fully developed mature personality)."

Remarkablewithin these developmental zones are the possible character formations with theirmanifest behavioral traits.

Impulsive children are certainly not easy to handle for teachers in school, as they tend to undisciplined reactions and often stand out due to their disruptions of the class. They either have an attention deficit or are simply immature or "uneducated," which indicates poor or inappropriate upbringing in their home. In individual cases, an "Attention Deficit Hyperactivity Disorder (ADHD)" as a psychologically induced attention and hyperactivity disorder associated with impulsive behavior is also to be assumed. ADHD issues with their pronounced attention and concentration deficits must be treated within the framework of therapy if necessary.

Defensive individuals tend to defensive attitudes and also to lying if it helps them, without feeling a "bad conscience" and without feeling sorry in any way. They are rather embarrassed when caught and proven to be lying, so that, to prevent worse, they are forced to tell the truth. Their manipulation potential thus lies in defending their own well-being against other people, especially authorities.

Conformists are supporters of "Law & Order," i.e., law and order, and are therefore particularly connected and inclined towards authority figures such as teachers. Towards classmates, they like to act as "guardians of law and order" and reprimand them when necessary. In extreme cases, they have the potential to become a "trained subordinate": "Bow to those above, kick those below!"

Mature personalities come quite close to the "master categories" postulated by deCharms (1979, p. 124) as developmental goals. These are the goals or behavioral maxims:

"a) internal goal setting;
b) internal instrumental activity;
c) reality assessment;
d) self-responsibility;
e) self-confidence;
f) internal control."

Noticeableor significant deficits in these listed developmental goals on the one hand, orremaining at a previous developmental stage on the other hand (e.g., as a defensivepersonality), can lead to offensive characters in interpersonal behavior and to ageneral lack of behavioral adaptation. In the case of a fixation on one of these"immature" developmental stages, further development into a "mature personality," especially upon reaching adulthood, would be rather unlikely or even excluded andimpossible.

Teachers are well advised in conducting their lessons if, on the one hand, they perceive these different developmental stages in their students and consider them in their teaching behavior, and on the other hand, as practiced in this research project, address social topics of "human interaction" with the students and have them describe and narrate them as short stories. Ideally, they pick up on such everyday episodes of the students in which these developmental goals occur and are problematized. In this way, educators can gain an enormous influence on the personal and social development of the students. Both on their attitudes and their behavior, the teachers would exert a great influence.

12.2 Methods of Educational Diagnostics

Most often, scientists in educational psychological studies use test procedures that correspond to the intellectual level of children and adolescents. The aim of the investigation is either performance assessments, which, if necessary, allow a prediction of learning or school success, or more psychologically oriented investigations with special procedures. Personality tests would be, for example, a method of data collection that concerns the attitudes of schoolchildren towards general or socially relevant topics or touches and concretizes their experiences with selected social situations, such as with teachers, classmates, etc.

Preferred data collection instruments in school psychology are "narrative" procedures, in which students are presented with a scene to which he (or she) should spontaneously invent a short story that reflects the current experiential background. Alternatively, specific questions, as in the "Thematic Apperception Test (TAT) by Murray (1943), can also be given to the subjects for an interactive scene (or a picture with a social background) to facilitate their response. Ultimately, this approach is very close to the projective psychological test procedures like the TAT, where subjects are shown a sequence of images with the associated guiding questions (cf. deCharms, 1979, p. 98):

"1) What is happening here?
2) What happened before or what preceded the scene?
3) What are the involved persons thinking or wishing?
4) How could it continue?"

Throughexperience-oriented episodes or short stories, the images are to be interpreted and, ifgiven, the questions answered.

Achievement motivation as a central motive for students originally thematized, for example, the following aspects or sub-criteria:

"a) Competition with an externally set goal or level of aspiration;
b) Intra-individual comparison with one's own abilities for the purpose of performance improvement;
c) Realization of a unique extraordinary achievement (e.g., invention);
d) Orientation towards long-term set goals (such as career development)."

Thesecriteria of achievement motivation also have limited relevance for schoolchildren.

In some exercises used within the framework of the research project under the leadership of deCharms, achievement motivation with all its associated facets could be well operationalized. Thus, in the "ring toss game" and a prior selection of low, moderate, and difficult requirements as a goal setting, the sense of reality of the schoolchildren, combined with their own level of aspiration, could be well observed and determined. In the "blind leader game," on the other hand, the participants were challenged to assist a "blind person" as a helper and to provide the blind person with measured support, security, and guidance so that the person being cared for gradually gained self-confidence and could act independently. Sensitivity to the necessary degree of influence was the central social requirement for the schoolchildren as caregivers in this game.

It is not at all surprising that a fantasy test was also designed and used for the relevant model "Master-Puppet," which, in line with projective procedures, encouraged the creation of "Short Stories." These short stories were then evaluated according to typical behavioral criteria to infer the currently felt emotions of the student (or the target person) (see deCharms, 1979, p. 117).

Overall, the characteristic aspect "internalized goal setting" was best suited to differentiate between puppets and their master (see deCharms, 1979, p. 124). Additionally, the sense of reality considering situational circumstances and the self-confidence that shone through and emerged in a desired positive outcome of the story served as distinguishing criteria.

Schoolchildren can be manipulated towards desired behavioral changes during lessons based on the observations made if they, on the one hand, have the freedom to think and decide for themselves what they could do next, and on the other hand, are given the opportunity to "playfully" try themselves and learn directly from the experiences gained in the "here and now" (see deCharms, 1979, p. 49).

12.3 Transfer to Other "Learning Groups"

In this context, transfer refers to the application of scientific findings from the school sector to adults, who are to be promoted in professional practice through seminars for knowledge transfer (or "skills") or other personnel development measures (i.e., PD measures).

Personnel consulting or coaching within the framework of PD has already been addressed earlier (see Sect. 10.3.1.2). Now, the focus is more on collective PD measures, such as seminars and training sessions, which are offered and conducted similarly to school, either in the form of lessons for imparting new knowledge or as behavior training for personality development. It must be conceded, however, that the topic of "PE" has already been extensively and comprehensively covered in the professional literature from all conceivable directions and under various aspects, so there should hardly be any potential for new insights!

Analogous to the school sector, this contribution deals with manipulations that are also virulent and entrenched in corporate training and further education. Often, employees are called upon to "convince" other people, be it colleagues, their superiors, or customers and suppliers, and to assert themselves with their concerns.

12.3 Transfer to Other "Learning Groups" 141

Their toolkit is then the entire arsenal of manipulation techniques to achieve their goals. Therefore, corporate PD must have a "toolbox" of influence methods that it offers for learning and trying out (e.g., handling objections in typical sales situations or dealing with scheduling difficulties, delivery problems, or complaints in customer service).

With regard to the various company-specific educational measures, an attempt should be made to distill the existing potential for manipulations and subject it to an assessment or diagnosis, as well as to discuss it for possible application. It is not necessary to repeat the already existing explanations on consultations, negotiations, and sales talks that occur on various occasions in the working world (see Sect. 10.3). Thus, a glance at the offered corporate seminars and the like is sufficient to capture essential aspects of manipulation.

For example, a popular educational measure in practice is the introduction of creativity techniques. Seminar participants learn in teams how to deal with new ideas, suggestions, or proposals from others; they should not be criticized, devalued, or rejected at an early stage when they are still undeveloped! On the other hand, they learn how the ideas or proposals of others can help them by being picked up, processed, further developed, and "refined." Manipulation and counter-manipulation occur as interdependent behavior among seminar participants as well as later in practice.

Leadership and personality seminars also contain a great potential for manipulation. Each seminar participant experiences feedback from both the other participants and the seminar leader, in addition to self-experience. With self-experience, for example, through a suitable exercise like the "fantasy journey" (see Wienkamp, 2021a, p. 119 ff.), which aims at a "journey" through certain past life stages, the individuals engage in a kind of self-suggestion by becoming aware of certain events from their past and confronting them. As mentioned earlier, a participant might remember, for example, that he (or she) would have preferred to become a teacher and, at the request of his (or her) parents, pursued a different career, which still causes him or her pain and distress today. Since such an event is irreversible, this person should come to terms with it and find peace. The "fantasy journey" exercise should help him (or her) through self-suggestion to overcome these still burdensome "traumas."

Partner exercises, such as psychodrama or role-playing, are suitable for mutual feedback and may lead to changes in attitudes and behavior. The effect may be further enhanced if a seminar participant receives a specific, clear feedback from the entire group. At the appropriate time, the seminar leader also intervenes with interpretations, explanations, etc., and influences the participants in his or her own way, for example, through "reframing."

Comparable, yet different in orientation from "rational decision models" (see Chap. 8) are scenario techniques, which are also frequently used in seminar practice against the backdrop of corporate strategy development and planning. However, scenarios are not about solving an optimization problem; they are meant to describe a possible future development under certain premises and to subject these planning models (scenarios) to a so-called "plausibility check," i.e., if necessary, a "premise critique." Seminar participants then learn how to moderate a planning commission or strategy group and how to handle the "creative" drafts and ideas, especially during the final evaluation and documentation. The potential for manipulation lies in binding the participants to their self-imposed goals and planning premises, which they should adhere to disciplinedly during the planning process.

"Dirty tricks," which lead to exercising manipulations secretly and covertly, are not part of the seminar program, as they counteract any authenticity of an individual and are detrimental to cooperation and collaboration within the company. At most, such practices can be pointed out as a precaution for the self-protection of employees.

Special personality tests for PD are known (see, for example, the anthology by Passmore, 2008) and have a helpful function in coaching, for instance, by generating and providing a "second opinion" on the assessment of personality through the test (see Wienkamp, 2021a, pp. 107 and 154 ff.), which can then be compared with the general impression.

12.4 Summary

Learning is essentially the most important element in our lives and an irreplaceable component of evolution. Without learned adaptation to the "harsh reality" and environment, survival is not possible.

Even during school years, efforts were made to explore the best conditions for learning, and thus also for the personal development of schoolchildren, through extensive studies. The result of these studies showed that only the internalization of learning material and situational personal experiences help further and guarantee the individual a "causal autonomy" as the highest learning goal.

The most effective method and practice is the so-called "emotional learning," which provides the prerequisite for storing affective learning experiences in the "emotional memory" and retrieving them as value judgments and behavioral maxims when needed. Teachers can help students develop into self-responsible and independent personalities with their pedagogical skills.

Ultimately, the degree of self-responsibility also depends on the motivation to perform in the form of willingness to learn and readiness to exert effort, but also on a reality-based perception and assessment of the available possibilities. The metaphor of this learning model was the concept of the "master-puppet relationship," which offered itself as a reciprocal life cycle model. Fixation in one of the ongoing developmental phases can mean a stagnation of natural development and maturity and lead to the formation of noticeable negative character traits that can persist into adulthood.

The method of choice for personality studies in schoolchildren is projective procedures, such as a "fantasy test," which requires the subjects to provide experience-relevant short stories.

12.4 Summary

Of course, these insights into the learning of schoolchildren can be partially transferred to corporate or vocational education with adults. In all types of seminars, such as creativity techniques, behavior, or personality seminars, etc., it is important that the participants gain a high degree of self-experience, which, just like with schoolchildren, imprints itself in their "emotional memory" and can be retrieved and applied when needed. Unlike in school, experiences accompanied by emotions in adult education have a different significance, and in the daily work environment, employees must constantly "convince" others with a lot of communication skills and influence to achieve their professional goals.

Lessons Learned 13

In the end, the question always arises, from which insights about the diagnostics of manipulations can we benefit and what can we take away as "takeaways":

1) Manipulations are indispensable and omnipresent in normal everyday life, because the motto applies: "You cannot *not* manipulate!" When social influences or manipulations occur everywhere and happen more or less involuntarily, it is all the more important in critical situations to recognize them, to diagnose them as what they are, in order to deal with them sensibly and appropriately.

In the past, there has already been an attempt to portray "manipulation as a system," since the individual facets or manifestations of manipulations are not uniform but appear in various forms. For example, anyone attempting to manipulate needs a victim as a target person who is willing to be influenced and thus fulfills the attribute of suggestibility, as a counterpart to suggestiveness. Additionally, the goal at this point was to concretize the complex of characteristics of manipulation in its different variants and manifestations as a behavior pattern. In addition to the first attempt to portray manipulation as a complex structure or system, an expansion of the "varieties" and manifestations of manipulative behavior to now a total of *seven* sub-types or characteristic facets took place. The system of manipulation methods was supplemented with the attributes: "disguise, deceive and hide" and "voyeurism." This diversification of social influence is advantageous, if only because a more precise description and distinction between the individual variants of manipulation is necessary and hopefully successful for practical use, e.g., between rather involuntary attempts at deception and conscious lying.

Manipulations have a bad reputation for a reason and are morally offensive and questionable to most people. This applies without restrictions to the hidden secret manipulation maneuvers, where something is insinuated to the target person—possibly even to their own disadvantage. In such hidden influences, it is obvious to assume that manipulators think and act selfishly and only have their own advantage in mind. Salespeople who try to push something onto a customer that he or she may not need are the best example of this.

2) Without wanting to sugarcoat manipulations as such, they also have positive and useful sides when it comes to recommendations, advice, suggestions, etc., which are helpful and beneficial for a specific purpose or a relevant person. One might think of consulting services per se or also the assumption of care or educational tasks, such as a coach towards athletes whom they want to challenge and promote to win competitions or medals. This also includes all coaching, therapies, or healing treatments for the benefit of the client or patient.

Manipulations actually take place in secret, but they can also occur both unconsciously and with full intent and usually to one's own advantage using all tricks and ruses. The reaction to influences can also occur unconsciously as emotional reactions or impressions, such as a spontaneously felt sympathy as a "first impression" when meeting a target person for the first time, as well as formally, e.g., as a recorded statement of a witness to the interviewer's questions. Of course, anyone can also consciously manipulate themselves, for example, to fall into a deep relaxation or trance state. Self-manipulation also includes the involuntary yielding to prejudices or other stereotypes and voyeurism as a hedonistic drive.

Perhaps not necessarily to be understood as manipulation in that sense is lying, where it is about deliberately deceiving other people by asserting false facts (which is, of course, nothing other than manipulation). Therefore, it is not surprising that psychology has been dealing with lying or "social desirability" for decades and some personality tests included or still include a lie scale. In parallel, criminology or forensic psychology introduced the lie detector test, which reacts to neurophysiological or bodily signals when the subject is under stress, which would naturally and expectedly occur when lying.

3) As a particular concern in the course of individual or personality diagnostics, the differential psychological aspects should be appreciated and highlighted. For example, when diagnosing a disease, it must be clear why it is undoubtedly this disease. A look at the present symptoms or findings should exclude all other or similar diseases in the exclusion process, so that in the end only one disease diagnosis remains. Differential diagnosis thus means nothing other than accuracy and precision!

For psychological constructs or personality traits, the same requirements apply in principle as in medicine when making a diagnosis. Here, however, experts speak of construct validity when it comes to the existence or proof of a specific personality trait. Such a personality construct should also meet certain quality criteria in the determination or measurement, such as reliability or stability of the measurement (this means reliability as a criteria), and of course also be content-representative and recognizable, thus meeting the criterion of content validity. Sometimes this personality disposition also correlates with an (objective) external criterion and meets the requirement of criterion validity. Ideally, a personality trait can be used and applied as a predictor for predictions or forecasts of the relevant external criterion and would thus even fulfill the quality criterion of "predictive validity."

For the construct of manipulation, this means that both the individual subforms of manipulation and their relationship to other psychological traits (e.g., Machiavellianism or egoism) must be clarified. This is most effectively achieved through empirical studies, by subjecting the behaviors (items) proposed here to statistical examination, analogous to the construction of psychological tests. For the existing lie scale, this has largely been done in the past, and a close relationship to the construct of psychoticism has been established.

As a kind of addition to differential diagnostics, it should be noted that personality types associated with manipulation, such as some peculiar characters described by Theophrastus from antiquity, are also relevant.

In the individual diagnostics of persons, where the statements of those affected as well as the statements of other involved parties are to be collected and documented, it ultimately comes down to separating facts from rumors or hearsay to arrive at a solid assessment. Narrowed down to the question: "What is fiction, and what is the truth?"

4) A completely different field, alongside personal diagnostics, is the diagnostics or analysis of *systems* and their *processes*, where multiple parties always interact and want to assert their interests mutually. Scientifically, it is about *strategic* thinking and acting, which takes place in the form of "games" or moves and can assume different forms or game variants.

Ideally, and while maintaining "rationality" in action, the participants try to find a balance of interests or compromise that embodies something like a state of equilibrium ("Nash equilibrium"), with which all sides can arrange themselves. Strategies that include a balance or fair or at least as balanced as possible distribution of advantages and disadvantages for both parties are nothing other than a "best practice solution" and as a "Nash equilibrium" are without alternative compared to all other possibilities. In non-cooperative, i.e., simultaneous games, the demands on strategic thinking and calculating are significantly higher, as the intentions or possibilities of the opposing side can only be speculated upon.

However, there are also playful confrontations as a sequential process, which either contain retaliatory measures as revenge for suffered grievances or where cooperation between the players is possible or even intended, for example, through communication.

Whoever "holds all the cards," i.e., has a dominant strategy, will also (shamelessly) play it out, because the desired and expected result cannot be prevented by the other side, no matter how the opponent reacts. However, such a comfortable situation is rather rare, so in many situations, the potential reactions of the fellow player must be taken into account.

This dilemma is particularly evident in the popular prisoner's game (also known as the "Prisoner's Dilemma"), which, due to the uncertainties of the co-defendant during the parallel interrogation, prohibits risky actions, such as not confessing and denying the act (while the other accomplice behaves cooperatively and speculates on a pardon with a confession). Therefore, in almost all game situations, both suspects made a confession to possibly benefit from the "crown witness regulation" and leave the matter behind without punishment. At least a milder punishment would be expected for both accomplices with a simultaneous confession of the accomplice. The possibility of denying the act was only gradually used by the two alleged perpetrators in the relevant investigations after several trial runs or game rounds due to the incalculable risk and the suppressed communication between them.

5) Unlike simultaneous game approaches, "commercial life" is more characterized and dependent on cooperative practices, so such social principles as fairness, balance of interests, or reliable compromises must also be considered. Either one side opens the game with a move and the fellow player reacts to it, or a negotiation proposal is made, which the other side must agree to if the negotiations are not to collapse and no one benefits. This would then be the well-known ultimatum game.

While in auctions or bidding both mercantile thinking and acting as well as emotional sensitivities shape the bidding behavior to acquire the "object of desire," such as a unique piece of art or collector's item, game concepts in the social societal as well as political-military framework pursue entirely different goals. For example, the adherence to and realization of the generational contract through a pay-as-you-go system is a social and societal concern, behind which the cooperation-based game "Tit for Tat" (or: "As you do to me, so I do to you") stands. In contrast, military deterrence through "second-strike capability" is intended to deter and prevent aggressors from "playing with fire," as it is commonly called, and to make them aware of the risk of so-called "brinkmanship," or the "game at the edge."

6) For the diagnostics and analysis of systems and their inherent processes, there are no instruments comparable to individual diagnostics, such as psychological tests (with or without a lie scale) or the lie detector test introduced on the basis of neurophysiological indicators and used in criminology. The method of choice for system diagnostics is observation, supported by recordings or documentation, whether through film recordings or interview protocols, such as in witness interrogations.

Less than an "examination," such as an X-ray in medicine, system diagnostics of games, which focuses on interactions or processes, is understood rather as a scenario technique and meta-analysis with a view to the game process and the relationship of the game participants to each other. Depending on the game version, the payoff matrices, usually represented as a "four-field table" with estimated or assumed utility expectations as values, describe the initial situation, while decision trees help to understand the process logic of the actors in sequential game moves, in both game or process directions, that is, both forward into the future and as a "backward strategy" with a view back to the initial situation or starting position, which would be critically appreciated.

The system analysis becomes more complicated when pure strategies with perfect or complete information cannot be employed, but rather mixed strategies that rely on probability assumptions or expectations. Thus, with different weighting of actions according to their probability or frequency, alternative game moves are always to be expected, which are to be calculated and taken into account together with the "counter-probability $(1-p)$." A game based on probability distributions can also extend over several instances, gradations, or rounds, which is associated with extensive calculation as a decision basis.

Depending on the moral-philosophical or societal standpoint, the calculations for decision-making among utilitarians aim on the one hand at absolute payoffs as results, and on the other hand at measures of change considering the status quo, as preferred and propagated by the proponents of the principle of equality.

7) Initially, the interest was to present and address the "classic" games established in research, such as the prisoner's dilemma or the ultimatum game (see Chap. 6), to gain a first impression. This discussion was mainly about the significance of the "Nash equilibrium" as "best practice" for conducting games. In contrast, system analyses benefit more from practically relevant game versions, such as a balance of interests in the context of damage regulation or dealing with "free riders" in the workplace, as the situational conditions and problems to be solved become concrete and noticeable (see Chap. 7). Similar to the Nash equilibrium, problem-solving in practical problems usually lies in compromise formation as a balance or equilibrium of interests for both parties.

Therefore, various cases or constellations that in some form strive for a balance of interests, whether out of court by private agreement and consensus or by proposal or comparison of a court, as a compromise solution, provide an illustrative insight into the practice of game theory. Damage regulations, such as in or after traffic accidents, are illustrative examples suitable for system diagnostics.

Particularly relevant in practice and well-researched in social psychology is the phenomenon of "collective non-responsibility," which negatively and worryingly manifests itself in "failure to provide assistance" in the presence of several people or spectators and has often been confirmed in practice. Unfortunately, both research findings and observations in everyday life agree that the more people are present, the less likely it is to expect an emergency call in the event of an accident, as each of those present tends to rely on the others.

Finally, phenomena occurring and lamentable in the work or business world, such as "free riding," which is negatively characterized by a lack of work effort and collegiality, and "cheating," when individuals or organizations do not adhere to agreements or votes and try to enrich themselves at the expense of others, are also suitable for a system consideration.

8) Closely related to hypothesis testing and communication technology for detecting correct signals (or conversely "false or blind alarms") is signal detection theory, an instrument that has also increasingly gained acceptance in psychology for the detection or diagnostics of human performance (e.g., sensory or concentration performance). In measuring or checking individual performance capacity, this procedure concerns the "balancing act" between processing quantity (or speed) vs. accuracy (or errorlessness), which can be read from the number of errors made or "false alarms." A high willingness to take risks for quick judgments combined with a very high or "tight" workload usually comes at the expense of work quality measured by the error rate. Finally, it should be mentioned that signal detection theory is also suitable for evaluating lie detector tests in criminology or forensic psychology and enjoys practical dissemination.

For system diagnostics, sampling methods are also suitable when it comes to generating uncertainties in a specific population group and deterring them from misdeeds such as tax evasion, and on the other hand, the portfolio technique for strategic planning, which presupposes or implies self-reflection or self-diagnosis. Strategy developments involve nothing other than answering the question: *Where* do we stand today in certain performance or strategy dimensions and *where* do we want to go in the future to be successful?

9) In "Rational Decision Theory," the focus is on optimizing decision-making, which is guided solely by one's own preference structure, represented as a feature profile of decision-relevant alternatives. It should be noted that the criteria and their manifestations within the profiles are often not easily comparable, and a rational approach must be found to solve this "apples and oranges problem." In management literature or economics, decision-makers or HR managers often have to solve these decision problems or dilemmas, for example, when it comes to selecting a job (or conversely, an applicant) or making a strategic decision such as "make or buy" in production decisions.

Such decision problems can only be solved through a rule-based system, by ranking or ordering and normalizing the individual attributes of the alternative objects from minimum to maximum, and by finding a procedural approach that is suitable for comparing different attributes or qualities with their manifestations and relates them to each other in their values, thus finding a common denominator for them to enable a comparison.

How system-relevant concepts can also be suitable for self-monitoring one's own activities and decision-making processes ex post can be demonstrated by the example of a retrospective review of a personnel selection process.

If the probabilities of occurrence for a defined event, such as the base or occurrence probability (a priori probability) for a certain expectation, are also to be considered in this calculation, this could be done using "Bayes' Theorem." With this approach, the "realistic" probability for a critical event (e.g., a malignant tumor) can be determined as a joint result, taking into account both the probability of the occurrence of this event at all and the quality or reliability of the test diagnostics. As "connoisseurs" of this method will certainly appreciate, this approach to probability calculation allows for a sequential, graduated procedure, i.e., starting with a vague or approximate subjective probability estimate, which is then continuously subjected to an "update" in light of newly gained insights and experiences, leading to better results or predictions.

10) While the more rational decisions in pursuing selfish goals and purposes, primarily in competitive situations or to solve a selection or optimization problem, follow the aspect or goal of personal benefit maximization, prosocial behavior with the attributes of fairness, empathy, compassion, justice, etc., is subject to *social preferences*, in which strategic intentions are also required and become effective. However, the decision-maker or actor does not primarily orient themselves towards their self-serving personal goals but aligns their strategic behavior with the social circumstances that also consider the needs and concerns of other

people. Behavioral influences thus stem both from social preferences and from the empathy felt for the situation in which other individuals find themselves.

Social or interpersonal interactions require an "open social stage" to observe and examine both the quality of relationships and the communication paths on different levels. Purposeful conversations, where something is at stake, are full of manipulation attempts, which are dependent on and initiated by competing interests and motives. Just as in game theory with the Nash equilibrium, social interactions also strive for balance, as imbalances are either perceived as relationship disturbances or disagreements and are felt as a problem or "imbalance" that needs correction or resolution in one way or another.

Among the societal and social achievements are certainly the so-called "social preferences," which, alongside personal preferences, significantly determine and influence our lives. Without fairness, the assumption of social responsibility, and emotional involvement in the lives of our fellow human beings, prosocial behavior would be impossible.

11) Consultations take place for various reasons, for example, to clarify financial circumstances and their perspective or to help companies with personnel selection, to name just a few examples. Common to all consultations is the more or less hidden potential for manipulation, which does not manifest in the form of clear instructions but is veiled behind recommendations, suggestions, etc., manifesting "softly." This also demonstrates the correctness of the guiding principle: "You cannot not manipulate!" In consultations, financial advisors or personnel consultants are not selfless beings (or confessed altruists) but pursue their own selfish business interests from various perspectives. Therefore, they have no hesitation or scruples in applying their "dirty tricks" with great finesse in communication with their clients to achieve success. In social consultations or similar, different requirements are sometimes placed on the consulting business, as they primarily have a "public mandate" to fulfill and are committed to the common good.

12) In regular negotiations, completely different communication rules apply than in consulting. It would be an oversimplification to speak here of a "pull and push strategy." This means, on the one hand, trying to coax the negotiation partner out of their shell and bring them to your side (e.g., by "playing off the wall" combined with offering the opposing party to make a first proposal), which would correspond to a "pull strategy," and on the other hand, resisting with all means (to "push") to prevent the negotiations from reaching a deadlock or a "dead point," as they would then be stalled and there is a risk of a breakdown (and ultimate failure). If the negotiations are in the final round and currently on the home stretch, a clear signal should be sent, and the necessary closing ritual should be initiated. Sales negotiations, if they are even provided for within a marketing mix, have (e.g., in "door-to-door sales") their own procedure and dramaturgy and are often hardly separable from a consulting service and product presentation when the buyer is still in the information or exploration phase and can choose the "best offer" from several providers.

13) Communication is entirely different in interrogations or witness questioning, either with suspects or eyewitnesses, than in negotiations. It should be self-evident that the roles of these two target groups are completely different and that the process and also the intensity of the interrogation or questioning differ noticeably. In the interrogation of suspected offenders, the criminal officers must be careful not to fall prey to any prejudices, e.g., due to prior convictions or similar, beyond all leading questions or other interrogation tricks, and also that they not only focus on details in the statements, i.e., on a sufficient level of detail and a chronologically plausible sequence, but also "read between the lines," which may indicate hidden or deliberately concealed evidence or clues. Additionally, in questioning, assessments, or interrogations, "feigning" or "falsifying facts" is to be expected.

The requirements for interrogation specialists also apply to witness questioning. In the case of incriminating witnesses, a credibility assessment by an expert is sometimes necessary to classify the statements relatively safely and objectively. Especially witnesses can stand out with "half-truths" or otherwise "wander," if they simply imagine having heard or seen something. Furthermore, it cannot be ruled out that witnesses also pursue their own interests, which contribute little or nothing to the truth-finding and an objective, realistic assessment. For the interrogation of defendants and witnesses, in particular, the reality—or the truth—often has two faces!

14) Therapeutic approaches with the aim of treatment differ from consultations, negotiations, or interrogations. Not the principle of mistrust, as especially in an interrogation, but that of trust is the decisive element or success criterion of the therapeutic relationship. Based on financial therapy as a multimodal approach of various therapy schools, it was possible to demonstrate in many directions how both the interplay of different techniques and methods and the cooperation of various experts can work. However, it should be absolutely noted and respected that a therapist, similar to a coach or supervisor, cannot fulfill their "job" without influencing maneuvers when it comes to overcoming resistance on the part of the patient or encouraging the affected person to adopt new behaviors or habits.

15) In professional work and education, it always depends on persuasive efforts if the set goals are to be achieved. Based on this ubiquitous goal, early studies in the school sector have ensured to determine which principles contribute both to successful learning and to a "mature" personality development. In educational research and developmental psychology, the dominant goal of an individual is considered to be the development towards "causal autonomy," which includes all relevant attributes such as achievement motivation, sense of reality, self-responsibility, and self-confidence.

Many insights and research findings from the school sector could be transferred to adult education and could be used in the program design of corporate seminars both to influence attitudes and to modify behavior.

16) Since manipulations are virulent in various social contexts or constellations and make themselves noticeable, it should be emphasized at the end that a "diagnosis of manipulation" should be conducted from different perspectives and with

their own approaches, and makes sense. Not only "self-awareness is the first step to improvement," but also external perceptions of current manipulations can protect against possible disadvantages or damages.

Moreover, it should also have become clear that manipulations encompass various fields of knowledge or research domains and therefore should not be treated and examined unidimensionally, but interdisciplinarily.

17) Do manipulations have a future? This could be the fundamental question at the end of this topic complex. Anyone who believes that a person cannot not manipulate would have to answer this question affirmatively, as the social phenomenon of manipulation, as highlighted in this contribution in various contexts, cannot be imagined away from our everyday life, let alone eliminated. Performing persuasive work, making oneself heard with one's arguments among other people, and asserting oneself, i.e., convincing, are some examples of our social interactions and indispensable means of communication.

However, it should also be demanded that in all social interactions and attempts at influence, certain behavioral norms and the commandment of fairness and truth or sincerity are considered and applied, so that on the one hand, the behavior with the underlying motives remains calculable for others, and on the other hand, no glaring disadvantages arise for them. Understood and implemented in this way, manipulation can succeed and would be "free" from criticism!

References

Adorno, T. W., Frenkel-Brunswik, E., Levinson, D. J., & Sanford, R. N. (1950). *The authoritarian personality*. Harper & Brothers.

Adshead, G., & Horne, E. (2022). *Warum Menschen Böses tun. Eine forensische Psychiaterin erzählt von ihren Fällen*. DuMont.

Arntzen, F. (1978). *Vernehmungspsychologie. Psychologie der Zeugenvernehmung*. Beck.

Arntzen, F. (2011). *Psychologie der Zeugenaussage. System der Glaubhaftigkeitsmerkmale* (5th edn). Beck.

Banse, R., & Gawronski, B. (2003). Die Skala Motivation zu vorurteilsfreiem Verhalten: Psychometrische Eigenschaften und Validität. *Diagnostica, 49(1)*, 4–13.

Berne, E. (2006). *Spiele der Erwachsenen. Psychologie der menschlichen Beziehungen* (6th edn.). Rowohlt.

Binmore, K. (2005). *Natural justice*. Oxford University Press.

Binmore, K. (2007). *Game theory. A very short introduction*. Oxford University Press.

Binmore, K. (2009). *Rational decisions*. Oxford University Press.

Brickenkamp, R. (1962). *Aufmerksamkeits-Belastungs-Test (Test d2)*. Hogrefe.

Britt, K. L., Klontz, B. T.,. &., & Archuleta, K. R. (2015a). Financial Therapy: Establishing an emerging field. In B. T. Klontz, S. L. Britt, & K. L. Archuleta (Eds.), *Financial therapy, theory, research, and practice* (pp. 3–13). Springer.

Britt, K. L., Archuleta, K. R., & Klontz, B. T. (2015b). Theories, models, and integration in financial therapy. In B. T. Klontz, S. L. Britt, & K. L. Archuleta (Eds.), *Financial therapy, theory, research, and practice* (pp. 15–22). Springer.

Canale, A., Archuleta, K. R., & Klontz, B. T. (2015). Money disorders. In B. T. Klontz, S. L. Britt, & K. L. Archuleta (Eds.), *Financial therapy, theory, research, and practice* (pp. 35–67). Springer.

Costa, P. T., Jr., & McCrae, R. R. (1992). *Revised NEO personality inventory (NEO-PI-R) and NEO five-factor inventory (NEO-FFI). Professional manual*. Psychological Assessment Resources.

Crandell, C. S., Silvia, P. J., N'Gbala, A. N., Tsang, J., & Dawson, K. (2007). Balance theory, unit relations, and attribution: The underlying integrity of Heiderian theory. *Review of General Psychology, 11,* 12–30.

Damasio, A. R. (1994). *Descartes' error. Emotion, reason, and the human brain*. Grosset/Putnam.

Davey, G., & Resnik, P. (2009). Die Grundlagen eines flexiblen, maßgeschneiderten Finanzplans. In O. Everding & M. Müller (Eds.), *Risikoprofiling von Anlegern, Kundenprofile treffend analysieren und in der Beratung nutzen* (pp. 85–112). Bankverlag.

Dawkins, R. (1978). *Das egoistische Gen*. Springer.

deCharms, R. (1979). *Motivation in der Klasse*. Lehrertraining und Unterrichtspraxis (Vol. 4). In R. Bauer & H. Hierdeis (Eds.). Moderne.

Dixit, A. K., & Nalebuff, B. J. (1995). *Spieltheorie für Einsteiger. Strategisches Know-how für Gewinner*. Schäfer-Poeschel.
Drucker, P. F. (2009). *Management. Das Standardwerk komplett überarbeitet und erweitert* (Vol. 1). Campus.
Düsch, E. (2001). Entscheidung für eine Fremdsprachenausbildung. In F. Eisenführ, T. Langer, & M. Weber (Eds.), *Fallstudien zu rationalem Entscheiden* (pp. 1–17). Springer.
Eisenführ, F. (2001). Berufungsliste für eine Professur. In F. Eisenführ, T. Langer, & M. Weber (Eds.), *Fallstudien zu rationalem Entscheiden* (pp. 133–152). Springer.
Eisenführ, F., Weber, M., & Langer, T. (2010). *Rationales Entscheiden* (5th edn.). Springer.
Engel, R. R. (2003). Stellungnahme zur Testrezension des MMPI-2 durch Hank und Schwenkmezger. *report psychologie, 28*(5), 304–306.
Eysenck, H. J. (1970). *The biological basis of personality* (2nd edn.). Thomas.
Eysenck, H. J. (1977). *Kriminalität und Persönlichkeit*. Europaverlag.
Eysenck, H. J. (1981). General features of the model. In H. J. Eysenck (Eds.), *A model for personality* (pp. 1–37). Springer.
Eysenck, H. J., & Eysenck, S. B. G. (1991). *Manual of the Eysenck personality scales (EPS adult)*. Hodder and Stoughton.
Fehr, E. (2009). Social preferences and the brain. In P. W. Glimcher, C. F. Camerer, E. Fehr, & R. A. Poldrack (Eds.), *Neuroeconomics, decision making and the brain* (pp. 215–232). Academic.
Gatewood, R. D., & Feild, H. S. (1987). *Human resource selection*. Dryden Press.
Glimcher, P. W., Camerer, C. F., Fehr, E., & Poldrack, R. A. (Eds.). (2009). *Neuroeconomics, decision making and the brain*. Academic.
Gray, J. A. (1970). The psychophysiological basis of introversion-extraversion. *Behavior, Research & Therapy, 8*, 249–266.
Gray, J. A. (1971). *The psychology of fear and stress*. McGraw-Hill.
Gray, J. A. (1981). Critique of Eysenck's theory of personality. In H. J. Eysenck (Eds.), *A model for personality* (pp. 246–276). Springer.
Gray, J. A. (1987). *The psychology of fear and stress* (2nd edn.). Cambridge University Press.
Gray, J. A., & McNaughton, N. (2000). *The neuropsychology of anxiety* (2nd edn.). Oxford University Press.
Hank, P., & Schwenkmezger, P. (2003). Das Minnesota Personality Inventory-2 (MMPI)*. Testbesprechung im Auftrage des Testkuratoriums. *report psychologie, 28, 5/2003*, 294–303.
Hathaway, S. R., & McKinley, J. C. (1943/1951). *The Minnesota Multiphasic Personality Inventory manual*. Revised. The Psychological Corporation.
Hathaway, S. R., & Meehl, P. E. (1954). Das Minnesota Multiphasic Personality Inventory. In E. Stern (Eds.), *Die Tests in der klinischen Psychologie* (Vol. 1, pp. 282–313). Rascher.
Hayos, A. (1972). *Wahrnehmungspsychologie*. Kohlhammer.
Heider, F. (1958). *The psychology of interpersonal relations*. Lawrence Erlbaum.
Holler, M. J., & Klose-Ullmann, B. (2007). *Spieltheorie für Manager. Handbuch für Strategen* (2nd edn.). Vahlen.
Jones, D. N., & Paulhus, D. L. (2014). Introducing the Short Dark Triad (SD3): A brief measure of dark personality traits. *Assessment, 21*(1), 28–41.
Kahneman, D. (2011). *Schnelles Denken, Langsames Denken* (2nd edn.). Siedler.
Kastner, M. (2001). Nutzenanalyse der betrieblichen Berufsausbildung. In F. Eisenführ, T. Langer, & M. Weber (Eds.), *Fallstudien zu rationalem Entscheiden* (pp. 89–115). Springer.
Klontz, B. T., Britt, S. L., & Archuleta, K. L. (Hrsg.). (2015a). *Financial therapy. Theory, research, and practice*. Springer.
Klontz, B. T., Klontz, P. T., & Tharp, D. (2015b). Experiental financial therapy. In B. T. Klontz, S. L. Britt, & K. L. Archuleta (Eds.), *Financial therapy, theory, research, and practice* (pp. 103–120). Springer.
Klontz, B. T., Horwitz, E. J., & Klontz, P. T. (2015c). Stages of changes and motivational interviewing in financial therapy. In B. T. Klontz, S. L. Britt, & K. L. Archuleta (Eds.), *Financial therapy, theory, research, and practice* (pp. 347–362). Springer.

References

Klose, D. (2000). *Theophrast Charaktere*. Griechisch/Deutsch. Reclam.
Kunkel, A., Bräutigam, P., & Hatzelmann, E. (2006). *Verhandeln nach Drehbuch. Aus Hollywood-Filmen für eigene Verhandlungen lernen*. Redline.
Lawson, D., Britt, K. L., & Klontz, B. T. (2015). Money scripts. In B. T. Klontz, S. L. Britt, & K. L. Archuleta (Eds.), *Financial therapy, theory, research, and practice* (pp. 23–34). Springer.
Lee, K., & Ashton, M. C. (2004). Psychometric properties of the HEXACO Personality Inventory. *Multivariate Behavioral Research, 39*, 329–358.
Leibetseder, M., Laireither, A.-R., Riepler, A., & Köller, T. (2001). E-Skala: Fragebogen zur Erfassung von Empathie – Beschreibung und psychometrische Eigenschaften. *Zeitschrift für Differentielle und Diagnostische Psychologie, 22(1)*, 70–85.
Levine, M., & Manning, R. (2014). Prosoziales Verhalten. In K. Jonas, W. Stroebe, & M. Hewstone (Eds.), *Sozialpsychologie* (6th edn.). Springer.
Malik, F. (1998). Anforderungsprofile – Eine Falle? *M.o.M. Malik on Management, Nr. 6/98*, (Eds. Management Zentrum St.Gallen).
McClelland, D. C. (1987). *Human motivation*. Cambridge University Press.
McCrae, R. R., & Costa, P. T., Jr. (1999). A five-factor theory of personality. In L. A. Pervin & O. P. John (Eds.), *Handbook of personality. Theory and research* (2nd edn., pp. 139–153). Guilford Press.
Murray, H. A. (1943). *Thematic apperceptive test manual*. Harvard University Press.
Ortheil, H.-J. (2022). *Charaktere in meiner Nähe*. Reclam.
Osborne, M. J. (2004). *An introduction to game theory*. Oxford University Press.
Passmore, J. (Eds.). (2008). *Psychometrics in Coaching. Using psychological and psychometric tools for development*. Kogan.
Plankl, W. (2014). *Theophrast Charaktere* (3rd edn.). De Gruyter.
Raiffa, H. (1970). *Decision analysis. Introductory lectures on choices unter uncertainty* (2nd edn.). Addison-Wesley.
Rokeach, M. (1960). *The open and closed mind: Investigations into the nature of belief systems and personality systems*. Basic Books.
Ruch, W. (1999). Die revidierte Fassung des Eysenck Personality Questionnaire und die Konstruktion des deutschen EPQ-R bzw. EPQ-RK. *Zeitschrift für Differentielle und Diagnostische Psychologie, 20(1)*, 1–24.
Rüdiger, H. (1949). *Theophrast Charakterbilder*. Dietrich.
Sages, R. A., Griesdorn, T. S., Gudmunson, C. G., & Archuleta, K. L. (2015). Assessment in financial therapy. In B. T. Klontz, S. L. Britt, & K. L. Archuleta (Eds.), *Financial therapy, theory, research, and practice* (pp. 69–82). Springer.
Schauer, F. (2022). *The proof. Uses of evidence in law, politics, and everything else*. Harvard University Press.
Schelling, T. C. (1960/2011). *The strategy of conflict*. Harvard University Press.
Singer, T. (2009). Understanding others: Brain mechanisms of theory of mind and empathy. In P. W. Glimcher, C. F. Camerer, E. Fehr, & R. A. Poldrack (Eds.), *Neuroeconomics, decision making and the brain* (pp. 251–268). Academic.
Spreen, O. (1963). *MMPI Saarbrücken. Handbuch zur deutschen Ausgabe des Minnesota Multiphasic Personality Inventory*. Huber.
Steinmann, K. (2000). *Theophrast Charaktere. Dreissig Charakterskizzen*. Insel.
Tuchman, B. (1962/2013). *August 1914*. Fischer.
Velden, M. (1982). *Die Signalentdeckungstheorie in der Psychologie*. Kohlhammer.
Watzlawick, P., Beavin, J. H., & Jackson, D. D. (1982). *Menschliche Kommunikation. Formen, Störungen, Paradoxien* (6th edn.). Huber.
Wienkamp, H. (2017). *The influence of incentive motivation and risk tolerance on risky decisions. An empirical study to show how direct effects from these psychological constructs and indirect effects from two mediators connected with risk, influence decision in ambivalent situations*. A thesis submitted for the degree of Ph.D., University of Nicosia, Department of Psychology.

Wienkamp, H. (2019). *Anreiz, Risiko, Ruin. Finanzpsychologie für jedermann!* Springer.

Wienkamp, H. (2020a). The influence of incentive motivation and risk tolerance on risky decisions. *Advance Research in Psychology, 1*(1). https://doi.org/10.46412/001c.13098.

Wienkamp, H. (2020b). *Der Weg zum Personalkennzahlensystem. Das HR-Cockpit in der Praxis – Einfach, pragmatisch, systematisch.* Springer.

Wienkamp, H. (2020c). *Psychologische Anforderungsanalysen in Theorie und Praxis. Für Führungskräfte und Personalexperten, die Anforderungsprofile erheben wollen* (Essentials). Springer.

Wienkamp, H. (2021a). *Psychologische Anforderungsanalysen. Anforderungsprofile für Management, Arbeit und Business.* Springer.

Wienkamp, H. (2021b). *Psychological requirements in theory and practise: For executives and human resource managers who want to raise requirement profiles* (Essentials and eBook). Springer.

Wienkamp, H. (2022a). *Manipulation als System. Über die bekannten und verborgenen Seiten systematischer Beeinflussungen* (Essentials). Springer.

Wienkamp, H. (2022b). *Strategische Personalbeurteilungen. Wirtschaftspsychologische Systeme für das Performance Management.* Springer.

Wienkamp, H. (2022c). Wen brauchen wir wirklich? Kein Recruiting ohne Anforderungsprofile. *personal manager, 6*(22), 44–47.

Wienkamp, H. (2023a) Manipulation – Oder, „man kann nicht nicht manipulieren!". *people & work 04/23.*

Wienkamp, H. (2023b). *Herausforderungen und Strategien der Personalberatung und Personalbetreuung – aus der wirtschaftspsychologischen Praxis, für die Praxis.* Springer.

Wienkamp, H. (in preparation). *Persönlichkeitstest über Ihr Business- und Finanzprofil. Der „Six & Six".* Springer.

Wilson, G. D. (1981). Personality and social behaviour. In H. J. Eysenck (Eds.), *A model for personality* (pp. 210–245). Springer.